AUTOBIOGRAPHY

THE SELF MADE TEXT

STUDIES IN LITERARY THEMES AND GENRES

Ronald Gottesman, Editor

University of Southern California

AUTOBIOGRAPHY

THE SELF MADE TEXT

James Goodwin

Twayne Publishers
New York

Maxwell Macmillan Canada
Toronto

Maxwell Macmillan International
New York   Oxford   Singapore   Sydney

Autobiography: The Self Made Text
James Goodwin

Studies in Literary Themes and Genres No. 2

Twayne Publishers
Macmillan Publishing Company
866 Third Avenue
New York, New York 10022

Maxwell Macmillan Canada, Inc.
1200 Eglinton Avenue East
Suite 200
Don Mills, Ontario M3C 3N1

Library of Congress Cataloging-in Publication Data

Goodwin, James, 1945–
    Autobiography: the self made text / James Goodwin.
        p.   cm. — (Studies in literary themes and genres; no. 2)
    Includes bibliographical references and index.
    ISBN 0-8057-0954-1 (hardcover)
    1. Autobiography—Authorship. 2. Biography as a literary form. 3. Self in literature. 4. Literature, Modern—History and criticism. I. Title. II. Series.
CT25.G6   1993
808'.06692—dc20   93-11948
                                                                                                                 CIP

The paper used in this publication meets the minimum requirements of American National Standard for Information Sciences—Permanence of Paper for Printed Library Materials. ANSI Z3948-1984. ∞ ™

10 9 8 7 6 5 4 3 2 1 (hc)

Printed in the United States of America

for Andrea,
and a life history together

General Editor's Statement

Genre studies have been a central concern of Anglo-American and European literary theory for at least the past quarter century, and the academic interest has been reflected, for example, in new college courses in slave narratives, autobiography, biography, nature writing, and the literature of travel as well as in the rapid expansion of genre theory itself. Genre has also become an indispensable term for trade publishers and the vast readership they serve. Indeed, few general bookstores do not have sections devoted to science fiction, romance, and mystery fiction. Still, genre is among the slipperiest of literary terms, as any examination of genre theories and their histories will suggest.

In conceiving this series we have tried, on the one hand, to avoid the comically pedantic spirit that informs Polonius' recitation of kinds of drama and, on the other hand, the equally unhelpful insistence that every literary production is a unique expression that must not be forced into any system of classification. We have instead developed our list of titles, which range from ancient comedy to the Western, with the conviction that by common consent kinds of literature do exist—not as fixed categories but as fluid ones that change over time as the result of complex interplay of authors, audiences, and literary and cultural institutions. As individual titles in the series demonstrate, the idea of genre offers us provocative ways to study both the continuities and adaptability of literature as a familiar and inexhaustible source of human imagination.

Recognition of the fluid boundaries both within and among genres will provide, we believe, a useful array of perspectives from which to study literature's complex development. Genres, as traditional but open ways of understanding the world, contribute to our capacity to respond to narrative and expressive forms and offer means to discern moral significances embodied in these forms. Genres, in short, serve ethical as well as aesthetic purposes, and the volumes in this series attempt to demonstrate how this double benefit has been achieved as these genres have been transformed over the years. Each title in the series should be measured against this large ambition.

RON GOTTESMAN

Contents

Preface

Within the genre autobiography the reader finds books by people from every conceivable walk of life: statesmen, poets, entertainers, scientists, laborers, royalty, military leaders, novelists, criminals, industrialists, deal-makers, activists, athletes, feminists, . . . ; the list is encyclopedic. The qualities of personality and of social experience represented in autobiography are also as diverse as one can imagine. The famous and the obscure, the rich, middle class, and poor, the arrogant and the modest, the saint and the sinner—all have used the genre to tell a reading public what they believe, and think the public should believe, is noteworthy about their lives.

The genre has contributed classic works to the world's literatures, and it has functioned significantly in the emergence of new literary voices from cultures that have been confined previously to minority status. The Chronology outlines the history of the genre's development as that history is recounted in Chapter 1. The "Overview of the Genre" in Chapter 1 examines important social, historical, and literary considerations related to the genre. From an account of the genre's characteristics, the overview moves on to key works in its literary history. The explorations in consciousness and memory that have evolved through the genre also have important counterparts in philosophy, psychology, and the social sciences. Examples of these counterparts are the subject of the chapter's conclusion.

As a consequence of the democratic revolutions in the United States and France, the genre autobiography is prominent in its contribution of both classic works and socially influential books to their two national literatures. In recognition of this cultural fact, and for the purpose of analyzing its implications, the autobiography texts selected for close study in the chapters that follow are drawn from American literature and French literature. In addition to its acknowledged masterworks, the genre has offered to individuals who might otherwise be excluded from the spheres of representation and publication the power to address society in their own voices.

Chapter 2, "Franklin's *Autobiography* and the American Mythos of Success," evaluates the meaning and the cultural legacy of the "conducting Means" Franklin employed to achieve success as a printer, merchant, writer, publisher, inventor, educator, and reformer. For posterity, the historical Benjamin Franklin is inseparable from the myth of the self-made individual that lives on in the autobiography. Adapting some concepts from Max Weber's analysis of Franklin and the social ethic of capitalist culture, this chapter concludes with a brief discussion of the American success story paradigm in autobiographies by P. T. Barnum, Andrew Carnegie, and Lee Iacocca.

Chapter 3 discusses the *Narrative of the Life of Frederick Douglass, an American Slave* as an example of the compelling relationship between literacy and liberation in African-American autobiography. The battle to achieve literacy in defiance of the strictures of slavery was the first stage of Douglass's freedom from bondage. In fact, an ability to read and write was instrumental in his plans for escape to the North. A distinctive cultural relation between language and liberation is found in autobiographies by Harriet Jacobs, Richard Wright, and Malcolm X, which are the focus of the chapter's closing sections.

Chapter 4 examines the questions of self that Gertrude Stein pursues in her two autobiographies. With *The Autobiography of Alice B. Toklas*, Gertrude Stein assumes the persona of her companion Toklas, whose domestic function was to entertain the "wives of famous men." Stein's use of the third person as a form of self-reference—a trait to be found in the autobiographies of Henry Adams and Sean O'Casey as well—creates a modernist objectification of experience. The style in *The Autobiography* is an exercise in "composition as explanation," particularly in the accounts of sitting for the famous Picasso portrait, of the cross-currents among the many important artists and avant-garde movements in Paris, and of the definitively modern nature of war in the years 1914–1918. In the subsequent *Everybody's Auto-biography*, Stein experiments with impersonal representation and considers the effects of a monetary culture on the value of self.

Chapter 5, "Montaigne's *Essays*, Rousseau's *Confessions*, Sartre's *Words*: Language and Self," compares three very different kinds of self-inquiry. Montaigne claims that the literary style in the *Essays* is a direct transcription of his thinking. With an analogy that conveys his humanist faith, he claims further that his life is consubstantial with the book itself. Rousseau's method in *The Confessions* is one of frank, literary narcissism. Rousseau develops a self-consciously "operatic" style to convey "all the extravagances of my heart." Sartre, in language that parodies the liturgy of Mass, portrays himself as a boy imagining that he will be reincarnated as a uniformly bound set of volumes. The transfiguration he imagines is not a religious mystery but rather an existential paradox. The self becomes *other*; the subject becomes pure object. Precociously, in becoming absent to himself before the literary career has even begun, the boy Sartre antici-pates the mature writer's greatest ambition, immortality and immanence. By comparison, Sartre represents a postmodern rev-olution in sensibility and identity, while Rousseau represents a modern one.

The final chapter treats two instances of the importance of autobiography in the assertion of cultures traditionally viewed as minority, marginal, or forbidden. Through autobiography Jean Genet offers himself to the public as a homosexual, criminal writer, and Violette Leduc offers herself as a social outcast. *The Thief's Journal* celebrates Genet's success in embracing the fate of criminality predicted for him as a juvenile. Writing serves Genet as a means to recuperate the margin of freedom of his life as a vagabond and homosexual. His autobiography is a profane testa-ment of sainthood that redeems experiences that often, in the first instance, brought degradation and anxiety. Leduc in *La Bâtarde* opposes her mother's presence and power to her father's absence and betrayal. Her autobiography recounts her search for an ideal matrilineal relation to a world defined by patriarchal authority and indifference. The texture of her writing in *La Bâtarde* records the complex double binds of a woman's experience.

Secondary sources in the Bibliographic Essay are chosen to represent the analytical and theoretical concerns of previous chapters. The survey of criticism concentrates on publications in book form that have appeared since 1980. It is divided into several primary areas: bibliography on autobiography and on criticism of the genre; definitions of the self; criticism on autobiography as a genre; the uses of autobiography in the social sciences; spiritual autobiography; women's autobiography; British autobiography; French autobiography; American autobiography; ethnic American autobiography; and contemporary theory on subjectivity and language.

In the section on Recommended Autobiographies, works have been selected to indicate range and diversity in the genre and to reflect topics developed in the present book. Given the extent of publication in the genre, any such list is necessarily limited in scope. Many of the autobiographies recommended are described further in the annotated bibliographies listed in the Bibliographic Essay.

The general editor of this series, Ron Gottesman, is a valued colleague and friend, and I am indebted to him for editorial direction, suggestions on revision, and his valuable critical insights. I wish to thank Sylvia K. Miller of Twayne Publishers for her comments and suggestions in the final phase of editing the manuscript. For the advice, bibliographical information, and secondary materials they provided, I am grateful to several colleagues at UCLA: Robert Aguirre, Michael Colacurcio, King-Kok Cheung, Kenneth Lincoln, and Richard Yarborough. Support for my work on autobiography has been provided through a UCLA Summer Faculty Fellowship, the University's Academic Senate research funds, and the Center for Humanities at the University of Southern California.

Chronology

399 B.C. Socrates delivers his *Apology* to the Athenian tribunal.

ca. A.D. 63 The letters and Stoic reflections of Seneca.

171–180 Marcus Aurelius composes his meditations, *To Myself*.

ca. 400 Saint Augustine writes his *Confessions*.

ca. 1294 Dante's *La Vita Nuova* ("The New Life"), a sequence of poetry and prose that is both an account of the poet's love for Beatrice and an apology for romantic poetry.

1436 The transcription of *The Book of Margery Kempe* is concluded.

1558–1566 Cellini writes *The Life of Benvenuto Cellini: A Florentine Artist*, which is published complete in 1728.

1565 Teresa of Ávila completes *The Life of Teresa of Jesus*.

1572–1588 Montaigne composes his *Essays*. Published originally in 1580, major expanded editions of the *Essays* were issued in 1582 and 1588.

1637 René Descartes, *Discourse on Method*.

1666   *Grace Abounding to the Chief of Sinners*, the confession by English Puritan John Bunyan; it is published in five more editions to 1688, the year of Bunyan's death.

1674   Earliest recorded use of word *self* in the modern philosophical sense of intrinsic identity that remains the same through varying states of mind and experience: "A secret self I had enclos'd within / That was not bounded by my clothes or skin," Thomas Traherne, *Poetical Works*.

1683   First documented use of word *biography*, by John Dryden in his *Life of Plutarch*, where it is defined as "the history of particular men's lives."

1725–1731   Giambattista Vico writes and publishes his autobiography.

ca. 1740   *Personal Narrative*, the confession by American Puritan Jonathan Edwards.

1766–1770   Jean-Jacques Rousseau writes his *Confessions*.

1771–1790   Benjamin Franklin writes his autobiography.

1788   Publication of Rousseau's unabridged *Confessions*.

1789–1798   Giovanni Giacomo Casanova writes his twelve-volume *Memoirs*, which receive their first complete publication in 1826–1838.

1796   The *Memoirs* by historian Edward Gibbon appear.

1798–1799   At age eighteen, William Wordsworth writes the first two parts of a verse autobiography that follows events from infancy to his seventeenth year.

1805   Wordsworth finishes the first thirteen books to his verse autobiography *The Prelude, or Growth of a Poet's Mind*.

1807   First documented use of word *autobiography*,
        by Robert Southey in the *Quarterly Review*, a
        British magazine.

1833   Publication of Johann Wolfgang von Goethe's
        Poetry and Truth.

1845   The Anti-Slavery Office in Boston publishes
        *Narrative of the Life of Frederick Douglass, an
        American Slave, Written by Himself*.

1850   After years of revision, Wordsworth publishes
        the final version of *The Prelude*.

1854   American writer Henry David Thoreau publishes
        Walden.

1855   *The Life of P. T. Barnum, Written by Himself*, the
        first of three autobiographies by the American
        showman. Frederick Douglass, *My Bondage and
        My Freedom*.

1856   French poet Victor Hugo releases his autobiogra-
        phy in verse, *Contemplations*.

1861   Harriet Jacobs, *Incidents in the Life of a Slave Girl*.

1868   First complete publication of Franklin's
        Autobiography.

1873   *Autobiography* by the English philosopher and
        social thinker John Stuart Mill.

1892   *Life and Times of Frederick Douglass*.

1895–1897   In prison on charges of immorality, Oscar Wilde
            writes his apology *De Profundis*, which is pub-
            lished in 1905.

1900–1905   Sigmund Freud publishes three major studies
            that draw extensively on autobiographical mate-
            rial in his development of a science of mind:
            The Interpretation of Dreams (1900), *The Psycho-
            pathology of Everyday Life* (1901), and *Jokes and
            Their Relation to the Unconscious* (1905).

1903   Jacob Riis, *The Making of an American*.

1907   *The Education of Henry Adams* is printed privately; the autobiography is published in 1918, the year of Adams's death.

1913–1917   Three books of autobiography by American novelist Henry James: *A Small Boy and Others* (1913), *Notes of a Son and Brother* (1914), and *The Middle Years* (1917).

1914   *My Childhood*, the first of three books of autobiography by Russian author Maxim Gorky, is published.

1916   Irish poet and playwright William Butler Yeats publishes *Reveries over Childhood and Youth* (1916), which is followed by two other books of autobiography: *The Trembling of the Veil* (1922) and *Dramatis Personae* (1935).

1920   *The Autobiography of Andrew Carnegie*. French novelist André Gide privately prints and distributes his autobiography *If It Die*, which is released to the public in 1924.

1927   Japanese writer Ryunosuke Akutagawa composes *A Fool's Life* a few months before his suicide. *Daughter of Earth*, by American journalist and radical Agnes Smedley.

1929   Mohandas Gandhi, *An Autobiography: The Story of My Experiments with Truth*.

1931   *Living My Life*, by American anarchist and feminist Emma Goldman.

1932   *Black Elk Speaks, Being the Life Story of a Holy Man of the Oglala Sioux*, reported by John G. Neihardt.

1933   Gertrude Stein authors *The Autobiography of Alice B. Toklas*.

1934   Henry Miller, *Tropic of Cancer*. Novelist H. G. Wells publishes his *Experiment in Autobiography*.

1937   Gertrude Stein, *Everybody's Autobiography*.

1939   *I Knock at the Door*, the first of six books of autobiography by Irish dramatist Sean O'Casey.

1945   Richard Wright publishes *Black Boy: A Record of Childhood and Youth,* but he withholds the second part of his autobiography, *American Hunger,* which is not published until 1977.

1946   Paramahansa Yogananda, *Autobiography of a Yogi.* Michel Leiris, *Manhood: A Journey from Childhood into the Fierce Order of Virility.*

1946–1948   Soviet filmmaker Sergei Eisenstein writes many episodes of autobiography, published as *Immoral Memories* in 1964.

1948   *The Seven Storey Mountain,* the spirtual autobiography of Thomas Merton. Theodor Reik's *Listening with the Third Ear,* the autobiography of a psychoanalyst.

1949   Jean Genet, *The Thief's Journal.*

1955   *Tristes Tropiques,* by French anthropologist Claude Lévi-Strauss.

1958   *Memoirs of a Dutiful Daughter,* the first of six books of autobiography by Simone de Beauvoir.

1961   Carl Jung, *Memories, Dreams, Reflections,* an autobiography based on Jung's principles of the collective unconscious and human spirituality. *Mountain Wolf Woman, Sister of Crashing Thunder,* reported by Nancy Oestreich Lurie.

1963   Man Ray, *Self-Portrait.*

1964   Jean-Paul Sartre, *The Words.* Violette Leduc, *La Bâtarde.*

1965   *The Autobiography of Malcolm X.*

1967   Vladimir Nabokov, *Speak, Memory.*

1968   Norman Mailer, *The Armies of the Night,* winner of the National Book Award.

1972   Nigerian author Wole Soyinka releases *The Man Died: Prison Notes,* his autobiography as a political prisoner.

1974   *All God's Dangers: The Life of Nate Shaw*, reported by Theodore Rosengarten, receives the National Book Award.

1975   *Roland Barthes by Roland Barthes*, the autobiography of a French critic who has widely influenced contemporary thought on language and culture.

1976   The Asian-American autobiography *The Woman Warrior: Memoirs of a Girlhood among Ghosts* by Maxine Hong Kingston.

1981   Wole Soyinka, *Aké: The Years of Childhood*.

1982   *Something Like an Autobiography* by Japanese filmmaker Akira Kurosawa.

1988   Gay novelist Paul Monette publishes *Borrowed Time: An AIDS Memoir*, which is followed by his autobiography *Becoming a Man: Half a Life Story* (1992), winner of the National Book Award.

1

Autobiography

An Overview of the Genre

A number of autobiographies stand securely as classics in their respective national literatures and among the great books in world culture. To give only a representative sampling, we can think here of Saint Augustine, *Confessions* (ca. 400); Jean-Jacques Rousseau, *Confessions* (written 1766–1770; first complete publication 1788); Benjamin Franklin, *Autobiography* (written 1771–1790; first complete publication 1868); Johann Wolfgang von Goethe, *Poetry and Truth* (1833); William Wordsworth, *The Prelude* (1850); Frederick Douglass, *Narrative of the Life* (1845); Henry David Thoreau, *Walden* (1854); Maxim Gorky, *My Childhood* (1914); Henry Adams, *The Education of Henry Adams* (printed privately 1907; published 1918); Gertrude Stein, *The Autobiography of Alice B. Toklas* (1933); Isak Dinesen, *Out of Africa* (1937); Simone de Beauvoir, *Memoirs of a Dutiful Daughter* (1958); Jean-Paul Sartre, *The Words* (1964); *The Autobiography of Malcolm X* (1965); and Vladimir Nabokov, *Speak, Memory* (1967).

Most commonly, autobiography is a prose narrative, but there are a few long poems that properly belong to the genre. A renowned medieval precursor to the narrative autobiography in verse is Dante's *La Vita Nuova* ("The New Life," ca. 1294), a sequence of sonnets, songs, and prose commentary that is both an account of the poet's love for Beatrice and an apology, or defense, of the romantic mode of poetry Dante has innovated. The two preeminent narrative poems that are autobiographies in the full modern sense are Wordsworth's *The Prelude, or Growth of a Poet's Mind* and Victor Hugo's *Contemplations* (1856). While definitions of the genre made in this introduction apply generally to autobiographies in verse, they do not account for the specifically poetic features of such works.

Understanding what qualities identify autobiography as a genre is not simply a matter of defining the term, though this is a necessary first step. Most readers are familiar with such definitions of *autobiography* as "the biography of a person narrated by that person" and "a biography written by the subject of it." Yet these primary definitions, taken from standard dictionaries, beg the question of what *autobiography* means, for they neglect to tell us what *biography* is. A comparatively recent term in Western languages, *biography* entered English through Greek and Latin; its first documented Western use appears in a Greek manuscript that dates back to the sixth century A.D. According to the *Oxford English Dictionary*, *biography* was first used in written English during the latter half of the seventeenth century. In that period, British poet and literary critic John Dryden defined *biography* in the preface to a translation of Plutarch's *Lives* as "the history of particular men's lives."

The definition of *autobiography* in the *Oxford English Dictionary* as "the story of one's life written by himself" generally describes books like Rousseau's *Confessions* and Douglass's *Narrative*, but it is inadequate where autobiographies like Stein's *Autobiography of Alice B. Toklas* and Sartre's *The Words* are concerned. Stein formulates her book as the life story of Toklas, but in it Stein—not Toklas—is the individual of greatest importance. Though Sartre was approaching sixty years of age at the time he finished *The Words*, the autobiography limits its scope to a self-portrait of his mental life only up to age eleven.

As a form of life history, autobiography is always incomplete. Unlike the biographer, the autobiographer typically does not have the capacity to encompass an entire life span. The time following completion of the autobiography remains unrecorded. The autobiographer can write a sequel, as did Douglass and Stein, but the closing period of life, which can extend years or decades, remains beyond the grasp of a person writing a history of his or her self.

A more inclusive ground for understanding the genre is to consider the components to the combinative word *auto / bio / graphy*.[1] The combining stem *auto* means self, self-acting, or self-caused. *Bio* derives from the root meaning in Greek: "mode of living" or, simply, "life." *Graphy* is another combining form; in English this is derived from Greek, with the root meaning "to write." By definition then, autobiography brings into direct association self, life, and writing, with each component in dynamic, reflexive relationship to the other two. This root definition does not require that *personal history* provide the shaping form for the interrelationship between self, life, and writing, though one long tradition within the genre is historical in function.

The term *autobiography* did not enter the English language until the end of the eighteenth century, the period of the American and French revolutions, which greatly advanced the cultural and political importance of the common individual.[2] Many individual self-studies and life histories were written before this revolutionary period, but the new term marks a significant shift in the meaning and direction of such literary practices. This shift seemed to require a modern term for a genre whose antecedents appear in classical Greek and Roman cultures, early Christianity, and the Renaissance.

Origins of Autobiography

One root of the genre, traced by the scholar Georg Misch back to antiquity, is the Western philosophical tradition of self-examination.[3] Self-examination is of particular importance to Stoic philosophy, and powerful literary accounts of it were left by the statesman and dramatist Seneca (4 B.C.–A.D. 65) and the Roman emperor Marcus Aurelius (121–180). In his letters and recorded reflections, Seneca directs his thought both inward to matters of conscience and outward to the matter of the world's moral condition. This dual perspective in a work of self-reflection evolves into a powerful resource for autobiography, as in the master-works by Augustine and Rousseau. In the volume *To Myself*, Marcus Aurelius devotes his meditations toward inner experience in an effort to reach understanding of the universal meaning in an individual's own life. This contemplative purpose is shared by later autobiographers like Thoreau and Thomas Merton.

The single early work in Western literature most commonly identified at the origins of autobiography is the *Confessions* of Saint Augustine. Written as an act of devotion to God, in the *Confessions* Augustine enumerates his youthful sins and recounts the moments of crisis and conversion in his life. In this manner, Augustine records the history of his secular life, and he honors the divine power of salvation over his soul. Religious purpose governs Augustine's decisions in selecting those events from his life that would best represent the experience of a Christian mortal—one unworthy of salvation but hopeful of receiving divine Grace. Once the account of Augustine's conversion to Christianity is concluded, his book turns to meditations on subjects such as memory, matter, and Creation.

Throughout the *Confessions* Augustine addresses himself directly to God. In effect, Augustine permits readers to overhear his admissions of guilt and his appeals for forgiveness. He does so in an effort to persuade fellow mortals to follow his example. Generally, as a form of autobiography the *confession* emphasizes moral, intellectual, and spiritual matters through its author's act of baring the heart, mind, and soul. The activity of intimate revelation in the confession is typically meant to induce the reader into the process of soul-searching. *The Book of Margery Kempe*, which was transcribed between 1432 and 1436 from spoken accounts, records such a process in the life of a medieval bourgeois woman.

Under the instructions of her Catholic confessors, Teresa of Ávila, who was canonized in 1614, wrote *The Life of Teresa of Jesus* (1565) to recount the awakening of her faith, the spiritual trials she endured, and the powers of prayer. With the Reformation, a record by the individual of the soul's progress became a central component of Protestant observance, as in the examples of the English Puritan John Bunyan's *Grace Abounding to the Chief of Sinners* (1666) and the American Puritan Jonathan Edwards's *Personal Narrative* (ca. 1740).

The sixteenth-century French lawyer, civic leader, and scholar Michel de Montaigne adopted an emphatically different perspective and strategy in writing about his own experience. In his *Essays* (literally, "attempts" or "efforts"), Montaigne addresses not God but rather humanity, writing of shared frailties and abilities. The essays, written in the period 1572–1588, are exercises in personal judgment made over matters of concern to every individual aware of life's complexity and significance. For Montaigne ordinary experience—in the form of ills he suffers, ideas he develops, emotions he feels, and books he reads—is a foundation for knowledge. Montaigne does not attempt to present a continuous or detailed narrative history of his life. Instead, he experiments with the materials of experience that life immediately offers in an effort to discover the nucleus of human existence. His method of discovery is to reflect on individual human conduct and on the shared cultural principles evident in society. Montaigne is a great innovator in the Renaissance human sciences in this self-investigation, with his life and thought serving as primary, experimental evidence. The humanistic principle underlying the *Essays* is that "each man bears the entire form of man's estate."[4]

With his *Essays* Montaigne renews for literature the *apology*, a form in classical rhetoric for philosophical explanation and the justification of one's beliefs. Socrates' *Apology*, delivered at his trial by the Athenian state in 399 B.C. and related by Plato, is the most eminent example from antiquity. In an apology, or *apologia* (the Latin term often used in English), the guiding intention is to vindicate one's own beliefs and actions, often in the face of official censure or public controversy. In contrast to the confession, the apology as a literary form implies no admission of guilt on the part of its author. The essential rationale of an apology is that the writer, in explaining the origins of ideas and opinions behind actions, will rectify inaccurate and unfair judgment over his or her conduct.

Benvenuto Cellini, another prominent European of the sixteenth century, wrote a very different kind of personal account in the years 1558–1566. The title of an early edition of his book gives some idea of its contents. Translated in part, the title reads: *The Life of Benvenuto Cellini: a Florentine artist. Containing a variety of curious and interesting particulars relative to sculpture, and architec-*

ture, and the history of his own time. Written by himself in the Tuscan language. Of humble family origins, Cellini begins his account with an explanation of the motive for taking personal experience as his subject: "No matter what sort he is, everyone who has to his credit what are or really seem great achievements, if he cares for truth and goodness, ought to write the story of his own life in his own hand."[5] The book's title page and this explanatory statement accurately describe the literary intentions that find expression in the *memoir*. The memoir can be defined as the recollections of a person involved in, or at least witness to, significant events.

In the memoir form there is typically an extensive concern with actions and experiences other than those of the writer. Cellini, for example, provides the reader with much information about events external to himself but that involve notable artists, aristocrats, and churchmen. The memoir, then, is distinguished as the narrative mode in which the individual uses the incidents of an active public life as a guide to understanding the cultural or political tenor of the times. It is the mode often adopted by diplomats, politicians, and military leaders to leave a record of their policies and public lives. A leading assumption for the memoirist is that the public record of an individual life is likely to be interesting and useful to both contemporaries and succeeding generations.

One of the most famous memoirists is Giovanni Giacomo Casanova (1725–1798), the ingenious Italian adventurer whose opportunism took him to the major capitals of Europe. In 1785 Casanova was made librarian at a castle in Bohemia, and for the last ten years of his life he wrote his memoirs. The twelve volumes did not receive their first complete publication until the 1830s. Of doubtful credibility in several personal matters, including the many sexual conquests he claims, Casanova's *Memoirs* are nonetheless invaluable as a record of his recollections and opinions on important historical figures among the royalty of Europe, including Louis XV and Mme de Pompadour, on fellow opportunists like Cagliostro, and on philosophers of the age such as Voltaire.

The confession concerns matters that are often independent of the immediate social determinants of the writer's life. In composing a confession, the writer bares the soul or the heart in an attempt to reveal those truths about the self that are intrinsic and, possibly, eternal. The apology conveys the writer's reasoned and mature ethical or philosophical position, often as a response to a critical political, intellectual, or spiritual situation. The memoir is recognized by its broadly historical scope. The writer utilizes the memoir form to document the social history in which he or she played some part. In some cases, however, the traditional moral and social imperatives of these three literary forms have served writers as pretexts for what are truly acts of self-aggrandizement.

These three categories of the personal account are not entirely exclusive or definitive. In Augustine's *Confessions* the narrative of his soul's individual progress toward God is accompanied by theological explanation on matters of Christian faith. The memoir by Cellini augments the record of his artistic career and the depiction of prominent people with revelations about strictly private matters. Most of the studies of the self written before the nineteenth century, however, can be adequately classified according to their predominant intentions into the categories confession, apology, and memoir.

Two aims are served in maintaining such a classification for self-studies published before the word autobiography appears. First, in doing so the reader follows distinctions made by the writers themselves and recognized historically by their audiences. Second, attention to the distinct generic intentions of these three antecedents to modern autobiography enables the reader to perceive the cultural context of the individual work. In sum, an understanding of the generic properties and promises of these forms provides a basis upon which to assess the integrity and effectiveness of a particular text.

By the opening decades of the nineteenth century, *autobiography* was applied to studies of the self published in that era. A new, more general term must have seemed necessary to identify books in which the conventional intentions evident in confession, apology, and memoir are fused or redefined. Biography had achieved its full status as an intellectual discipline in the course of the previous century, and the biographical method had become an integral part of the inquiry into history. With the cultural emergence of biography, that of autobiography inevitably followed. Ironically, however, a number of autobiographers make no claims to historical significance for their self-studies. These autobiographies are written in the conviction that individual experience, regardless of one's achievements or failures, constitutes in and of itself an invaluable source of knowledge. Thoreau begins *Walden*, for example, with an expression of this belief framed in ironic modesty: "I should not talk so much about myself if there were any body else whom I knew as well. Unfortunately, I am confined to this theme by the narrowness of my experience."[6]

Modern Meanings of Self

Though many autobiographers continue to follow a primary, defining purpose of confession, apology, or memoir, other autobiographers believe that an account of one's own life is intrinsically worthy of public attention because the individual is of intrinsic worth. This outlook marks a revolution in the political and cultural value of individual experience in Western societies. By the onset of the nineteenth century, then, an absolute spiritual, philosophical, or social imperative was no longer a necessary precondition to the act of an individual writing an account of the self.

Two books that stand prominently as the threshold to the modern meanings of autobiography are Rousseau's *Confessions* and Benjamin Franklin's *Life*, which are subjects of extended discussion in later chapters. Originally published only in part under the title *Mémoires* (1791) in French and *Life* (1793) in English, the Franklin narrative was given its now standard title *Autobiography* in 1868 upon its first complete publication. Though the title "Autobiography" was not yet available to Rousseau or Franklin, their books exemplify the modern attributes that now centrally define the genre. Rousseau opens the *Confessions* with a grand overture to the singularity of his personality and experience:

> I have resolved on an enterprise which has no precedent, and which, once complete, will have no imitator. My purpose is to display to my kind a portrait in every way true to nature, and the man I shall portray will be myself.
>
> Simply myself. I know my own heart and understand my fellow man. But I am made unlike any one I have ever met; I may be no

better, but at least I am different. Whether Nature did well or ill in breaking the mould in which she formed me, is a question which can only be resolved after the reading of my book.[7]

In telling his life history, Rousseau applies what he considers the highest standard of truth, the standard of a "sensitive heart" (*Confessions*, 19). Rousseau composed the *Confessions* in the conviction that his unique personality consists in the priority of feeling over reason, the importance of inner truth over worldly success, and the unprecedented endeavor of displaying himself as he actually was.

Through the intimacy of his self-portrait, Rousseau puts the reader in the position of a juror weighing the credibility of the book and thus assessing the integrity of the man. In such regards, Rousseau's *Confessions* differs immensely from Saint Augustine's. Augustine appeals to God as the Judge on earth and in Heaven. He makes confession publicly so as to encourage fellow mortals to follow his spiritual example. For Rousseau, in contrast, confession is obviously not an act of humility or worship. In passing, Rousseau mentions man's "Sovereign Judge" at the outset, but he does so with an obvious tone of independence and pride (*Confessions*, 17). Rousseau's direct appeal is to the reader's individuality, and he makes it in full confidence that the *Confessions* reveals the unique person he knows himself to be. In effect, his book challenges its audience to equal Rousseau in frankness and the complexity of his humanity.

Franklin had gained international recognition by the time he began to write his autobiography, upon which he worked in four separate stages during the last nineteen years of his life. At the time of his death in 1790 Franklin had recounted his life history only up to 1757, the starting point of his great diplomatic career as the representative in Europe of American interests. Nevertheless, the opening statement to his *Autobiography* places the "Poverty and Obscurity" of his early years firmly in the perspective of the "State of Affluence and . . . Degree of Reputation" he enjoyed in the period when he starts his book.[8] Franklin recreates experience in the image of a humanity defined by its rationality and inventiveness. Instead of the inner truths that preoccupy Rousseau, Franklin devotes his narrative to the "conducting Means" he employed to achieve success as a printer, merchant, writer, publisher, inventor, educator, and civic re-former (Franklin, 1). Franklin's greatest achievement is his inven-tion of an individuality of broad social, political, and cultural consequence. Autobiography proclaims itself as a genre in the era when figures like Rousseau and Franklin assert a new indi-viduality in human experience.

Origins of the modern meanings of *self*—and of the closely related terms *individual* and *personality*—date back no earlier than the seventeenth century. Self is a relatively recent "category of the human spirit," to employ a phrase by the anthropologist and sociologist Marcel Mauss.[9] The centrality of self in the mod-ern world has reformulated old cultural and political issues and has posed new ones. The self as a social category has had formative influences on many currents within anthropology, history, linguistics, and psychology, themselves all modern dis-ciplines of knowledge. Autobiography—as a genre at the conflu-ence of self, life, and writing—is a literary record of human evo-lution in individuality.

Temporality and Memory

In clarifying the characteristics of autobiography further, it is necessary to distinguish the genre from other types of immedi-ately personal writing. The *diary*, the *journal*, and *letters*—while they share with autobiography direct representation of the writer's experience—differ from the narrative conventions typi-cal to the genre. As narrative, autobiography entails relationships within the writer's experience and identity structured or pat-terned by the passage of time. A diary, journal, or personal letter is usually not written with publication in mind (though there are notable exceptions), and none of them promise an inherent shaping narrative or distinguishing theme. These three kinds of writing typically contain spontaneous thoughts, unintegrated information on or description of persons and experiences, and notations about encounters or events soon after their occurrence. Though they provide historians and biographers with an invalu-able resource, as literary forms the diary, the journal, and letters do not share with autobiography the necessary temporal perspective, a deliberate distancing of the self from the original experiences. Ordinarily, these three forms do not embody the enduring qualities of experience that the passage of time makes distinct for the autobiographer.

Autobiography is retrospective. In most instances this property is obvious, but in some cases retrospection is conducted at a provisional, implied, or latent level. An autobiography represents the writer's effort, made at a certain stage of life, to portray the meaning of personal experience as it has developed over the course of a significant period of time *or* from the distance of that significant time period. Thoreau's *Walden* offers an effective demonstration of the definitions and distinctions being made here. As he did throughout his adult life, Thoreau kept a journal that amply records his daily experience during the stay at Walden Pond in 1845–1847. In the seven years between the experience itself and the publication of *Walden*, Thoreau composed and steadily revised the manuscript, which drew frequently from his own journal entries. His autobiography opens, "When I wrote the following pages, or rather the bulk of them, I lived alone in the woods" (*Walden*, 1). The past tense and the mode of retrospection evident here, however, are not consistently maintained in the narrative. Characteristically, they give way to the present tense and a mode of continuous actuality. The distance in time from the original experience, the book's retrospective dimension, has provided Thoreau with a philosophic awareness of the universality and timelessness of that experience.

Though Thoreau's stay in the woods lasted two years and two months, *Walden* does not narrate the experience in a chronological or historical manner. Instead, his autobiography refashions this passage of time into one cycle of the four seasons, from the spring in which he made preparations for residence at Walden, which he began on 4 July 1845 for its symbolic meaning, onward to autumn, winter, and the very first indications of the next spring. This classic work in the genre illustrates the fact that the narrative dimension and temporality of autobiography need not be chronological or historical in type.

The writer who sets about recounting a personal past does so in the recognition that the creative powers of imagination and memory (as contrasted with mere recall) are akin in several respects. In the first place, the mind does not record experience with complete objectivity or faithfulness. Moreover, the past cannot be recalled totally. The past evades complete recapture, especially as it recedes further back in time. Memory reconstructs and recreates, often more with an eye toward the present moment of remembering than toward the past experience remembered.

Walt Whitman is an autobiographer whose regard for the past is always incorporated within larger, vivid sensations of the present and a vision of the future. In "Song of Myself" (1855), his celebration of individuality and democracy, Whitman separates "the Me myself" from past personal experience:

> Apart from the pulling and hauling stands what I am,
> Stands amused, complacent, compassionating, idle, unitary. . . .
> Backward I see in my own days where I sweated through fog with
>   linguists and contenders,
> I have no mockings or arguments, I witness and wait.[10]

This long poem is structured by Whitman's imaginative processes of identification, expansion, and projection rather than by a narrative or a line of argument. The poem suspends prior experience and knowledge in favor of the immediacy of the present and the promise of the future:

> It is time to explain myself—let us stand up.
> What is known I strip away,
> I launch all men and women forward with me into the Unknown.
> The clock indicates the moment—but what does eternity indicate?
>   (*Leaves*, 61)

Typically, narrative progression within an autobiography is intended to convey a law of causality that itself dates from the past experience recalled. In "Song of Myself," the principles of consciousness and causality are instead transcendent of time.

Fact and Imagination

The powers of imagination and invention can be as important to the autobiographer as they are to the novelist, dramatist, or poet. Indeed, the autobiographer commonly uses the same techniques of fiction and drama to shape personal experience into meaning-ful narrative. In rendering places and people from the past, even when it is possible to revisit them, the autobiographer often applies imaginative and metaphoric coloration in order to bring them to life. When, as in many cases, conversation cannot be recalled in detail, the autobiographer creates dialogue to recreate the actuality of the past.

The following passage, taken from the opening chapter of *In the World* (1916), the second in a sequence of three autobiographies by the Russian literary figure Maxim Gorky, employs a number of devices shared with fiction:

> It was as a door boy in a smart, main street shoe store that I went out into the world. The boss was a tubby little man with a coarse, brown-ish face, greenish teeth, and moist, slime-covered eyes. I though he was blind, and, as a test, I made a face, at which he said with a rather gentle severity, "Stop twitching!" I was irked at the thought of those dead eyes watching me. Wasn't it more likely he had guessed I was making faces?
>
> "I told you to stop twitching!" he repeated, barely moving his grubby lips. "Stop scratching," his dry whisper stole, as it seemed, upon me. "You're working in a first-class store, just bear that in mind. The door boy must stand straight as a statue."[11]

He was no more than ten years old at the time of this incident. Yet Gorky was in his forties when he wrote this volume of his autobiography. Thus it is unlikely that he could recall the shop-keeper's precise words. Based on his recollection of the incident, however, Gorky creates dialogue and description that vividly reflect his reactions to the experience. The characterization is exaggerated through grotesque details to convey the frightening impression made on the child by the boss.

In fiction the convention of the narrator who writes in the first person and tells the history of his or her life is nearly as old as the novel form itself. In 1719, for example, English novelist Daniel Defoe published a book whose title page provided no clue that the contents were fictional or that he was its author. Its descrip-tive title reads, in part, *The Life and Surprizing Adventures of Robinson Crusoe, . . . Written by Himself.* Defoe in his own name addresses the reader directly in the book's preface, but he does so under the guise of being the editor of the original manuscript reputedly written by Robinson Crusoe. Defoe and other writers in the early generations of English novelists regularly used first-person narrative and related personal modes of writing—like the journal (Defoe's *A Journal of the Plague Year*, 1722) and letters (Samuel Richardson's *Clarissa, or The History of a Young Lady*, 1748)—to sustain an illusion of reality in their books. While some among the first readers of these novels may have thought they contained real-life stories, contemporary publishing practices ordinarily make clear the actual authorship of such first-person fictions by naming the novelist prominently on the title page.

Northrop Frye, an important literary theorist on the matter of genre, finds that autobiography "merges with the novel by a series of insensible gradations. Most autobiographies are inspired by a creative, and therefore fictional, impulse to select only those events and experiences in the writer's life that go to build up an integrated pattern."[12] A number of modern masterworks in the novel meld autobiography into fiction. A famous example, epic in its scope, is the sequence of novels *A la recherche du temps perdu* by Marcel Proust. Published in the period 1913–1927, the series title means literally "In Search of Lost Time"; the title in the English translation is phrased *Remembrance of Things Past*. Through a narrator named Marcel, Proust renders in these books a personal account of experience and, centrally, of the evolution of a writer's consciousness. The novelists Thomas Mann in *Buddenbrooks* (1901), D. H. Lawrence in *Sons and Lovers* (1913), James Joyce in *A Portrait of the Artist as a Young Man* (1916), and Thomas Wolfe in *Look Homeward, Angel* (1929) also trace the development of an artist's personality and work over a fictionalized life that contains close parallels with their own actual lives. These books belong to the literary type known as *kunstler-roman*, a novel about the development of an artist.

Other writers in the modern period have actively sought through autobiography to dislodge fiction as the dominant prose form. Henry Miller, to take one notable example, published his first book after years of futile attempts as a fiction writer. That book, *Tropic of Cancer* (1934), is the autobiography of a failed novelist, and it opens with an inscription drawn from the journals of Ralph Waldo Emerson, the American poet, essayist, and transcendentalist. In the cited journal entry for 1841, Emerson had stated, "These novels will give way, by and by, to diaries or autobiographies—captivating books, if only a man knew how to choose among what he calls his experiences that which is really his experience, and how to record truth truly." In his quest for authentic expression of the truth, Miller renounces literary refinement: "This is not a book. This is a libel, slander, defamation of character. . . . This is a prolonged insult, a gob of spit in the face of Art, a kick in the pants to God, Man, Destiny, Time, Love, Beauty."[13] Over the subsequent forty-five years of his writing career, Miller maintained his commitment to autobiography as the most powerful instrument of human truth.

Several contemporary forms of writing have sought to bridge or in some cases dissolve any boundaries between autobiography and fiction. The French novelist and critic Jean Thibaudeau identifies a strong tendency since World War II, particularly in the *nouveau roman* (or "new novel" associated with writers such as Alain Robbe-Grillet and Marguerite Duras), to compose "the novel as autobiography," with the writer and the writing process as its subject.[14] In writing narratives based on candid details of his personal life, the American writer Frederick Exley has applied the term "fictional memoir" to categorize *A Fan's Notes* (1968) and *Pages from a Cold Island* (1975). The novelist Norman Mailer has made himself, in the role of novelist, the autobiographical subject of several prose collections and narrative works, including *Advertisements for Myself* (1959) and *The Prisoner of Sex* (1971). His book *The Armies of the Night* (1968), subtitled "History as a Novel, The Novel as History," is narrated in the third person yet features as its protagonist Norman Mailer, whose actual political activities are reported through this narrative. Such narrative strategies, as practiced by Mailer, Tom Wolfe, Hunter Thompson, Michael Herr, and others, produce a contemporary prose form called New Journalism, which brings reporter and events into an autobiographical relationship that provides the story line for an experiential account of events.

The uses in autobiography of resources commonly associated with the novel and the fusion of autobiography with fiction by some writers, while complicating matters, does not finally make it impossible to draw categorical distinctions between the two genres. Philippe Lejeune is the literary theorist who has devoted the most attention to this matter.[15] For Lejeune the textual property that most distinguishes autobiography from fiction is in the form of a pact or contract between an autobiography and the reader, a pact initiated from the attribution of authorship on the autobiography's title page and onward through the book. The book's dimensions of self-reference have, through the autobiographer's proper name, verifiable referents in society and in history. In the genre's dominant tradition of first-person narrative, the same identity is distinctly shared by author, narrator, and protagonist. Narrative in autobiography is thus the self-referential enactment and identification among these three constituents of self in the text.

In Lejeune's approach to a generic definition, autobiography "is a mode of reading as much as it is a type of writing; it is a historically variable *contractual effect*" (Lejeune, 30). In the act of reading, the reader applies different sets of standards and expectations to suit the varied kinds of print material typically read. These standards and expectations are formulated and refined as the reader matures and grows more fully conscious of the interrelationships among language, the genres of writing, and reality. Autobiography narrated in the third person—a mode far less common, but one used in major examples of the genre, as in the life stories of Henry Adams, Gertrude Stein, and Sean O'Casey—presents a challenging redirection of the reader's expectations of person and perspective. This particular variation in the conventions and contract of autobiography is examined in the chapter on Stein that follows.

The Self-Life-Writing Dynamic

I have been arguing, then, that the combinative terms of autobiography—self, life, and writing—offer the grounds for a dynamic definition of the genre in terms of the text. A dynamic definition is useful in light of the fact that genre, like other forms of culture, is subject social, and ultimately historical, permutation and recombination. Thus, as the terms self, life, and writing shift and develop in meaning, the genre autobiography enlarges its boundaries and characteristics.

Two primary poles of language use, first identified by linguist Emile Benveniste and elaborated by literary theorist Gérard Genette, are *discourse* and *narrative*. In the major Western languages, discourse activates self through uses of the first-person forms of address. The first-person singular pronoun is unique in its language functions in that it refers to the act of speech or writing that contains *I*. It is precisely in this act, as Benveniste observes, that "the speaker proclaims himself as the 'subject.'"[16] *I* has no conceptual or universal meaning outside its concrete use in language. This circumstance allows *I* always to be available for every writer and speaker in the language. Thus the first-person pronoun singular possesses a context and a referent only in the act of discourse that contains *I*.

Discourse is the linguistic means of existence for individual subjectivity. As a convention of language use, *narrative is in contrast a dimension of objectivity*, defined by the absence of any reference to the writer or speaker. Pure narrative excludes personal expression on the part of the writer or speaker. The practices of narration common to the writing of history are a familiar example of this objective, impersonal mode. A history text typically omits the historian from its narrative of past events. The text excludes the time and place of the historian—the context of the historian's *discourse*, in other words—as he or she writes history.

Though in theory discourse and narrative are opposite dimensions of language, in practice typically one dimension is present in a subordinate role in forms of communication dominated by the other dimension. In the case of a history text, for example, the historian's explanation of method is an instance of discourse within a dominant narrative. For the genre autobiography, there is a necessary, manifest, and interactive relationship between discourse and narrative. This textual relationship is most obvious in the first-person conventions of autobiography, but it is ultimately no less true in the genre's third-person forms of narration. In autobiography there is the promise and expectation that the author's personal discourse functions in direct relationship with the narrative, while in the novel form there is not. The representation of self and identity through language, the linguistic property of discourse, is in autobiography constituted through the methods of narration and description. The alliance between discourse and narrative in autobiography aligns and clarifies the interwoven pattern of self, life, and writing that constitutes a text of autobiography. The individuality of each such textual pattern is the focus of attention in the chapters that follow.

Gender and Ethnic Issues

Autobiography has made significant contributions to social history and political thought, for it offers to individuals otherwise excluded from the spheres of political representation and publication the opportunity to address the public in their own voices. The genre has been of fundamental importance to the women's movement and to formulations about the distinctness of women's literature. Since gender has functioned in Western history as a basis for social differentiation and legal determination, it follows that the genre issues of identity, experience, and representation in women's autobiographies are engaged with larger issues of culture and politics. My discussion turns directly toward these matters in Chapter 6 and in the Bibliographic Essay.

The question of gender as a determinant of self and consciousness is also essential in autobiography by homosexual men and women. Martin Duberman's *Cures: A Gay Man's Odyssey*, for example, recounts a series of therapeutic experiences intended to cure him of his "disorder," and it relates his ultimate progression toward self-understanding and self-acceptance. In the civil rights activism of the gay movement, as in earlier political movements, autobiography has served the cause of personal and social liberation.

Cultivated and intimate self-consciousness has a long tradition in French autobiography, and it is turned toward previously taboo matters of sexual identity in books by Jean Genet and Violette Leduc, who are the focus in my concluding chapter of close analysis. Rousseau's *Confessions* set a precedent for frankness and unsparing private detail in this tradition. In *Manhood* (1946), Michel Leiris examines the development of his sexuality from childhood and confronts the troubled yet exalted experiences surrounding the matter of his own virility. With *The Thief's Journal* (1949), Genet uses autobiography as a means to gain a margin of freedom in his life as a vagabond, prisoner, and homosexual. The book explores the erotic intensity of a life condemned for its criminality and sexuality. In *La Bâtarde* (1964), Leduc treats as essential to adult identity her existence as the illegitimate daughter of a respectable man who refused to acknowledge her as his child.

In the course of its history as a genre, autobiography has demonstrably served to democratize the world of letters. In

American society, for instance, autobiography provided for African-Americans and for women forms of cultural enfranchisement before political enfranchisement was established in law. In the era of the American Civil War, personal narratives by Frederick Douglass, Harriet Jacobs, and other escaped slaves served greatly to mobilize Northern opinion in favor of abolition. The social influence of African-American autobiography is considered further in the chapter on Douglass's *Narrative*. In twentieth-century America the social conditions of women, the poor, the laboring class, minorities, and Native Americans have been brought to national attention by the urgent eloquence in autobiographies by individuals like Agnes Smedley, Emma Goldman, Jacob Riis, Nate Shaw, Richard Wright, Black Elk, and Mountain Wolf Woman.

The development of recording equipment in this century has made possible the transcription of life histories told by individuals who in previous centuries would never have reached a reading public. The media have made modern audiences recognize that some people who have no effective command of written English are nevertheless articulate and accomplished speakers of the language. Anthropologists and sociologists widely employ this technology to gather information about cultures and social groups based in oral traditions. Theodore Rosengarten applied such methods of field work in compiling the life story of Nate Shaw, an African-American tenant farmer and union activist born in the segregated South during Reconstruction. Though Nate Shaw was unable to read or write, the language recorded in his autobiography is that of an individual keenly observant of the world around him and eloquent in his understanding of life.

The Scope of the Genre

Important autobiographies, unlike the masterworks of some other literary genres, have been created by people in a surprisingly wide range of fields. Of course, the imaginative writer is especially qualified to endow personal experience with a conception of wholeness and intrinsic order or one of drama and conflict. Goethe's *Poetry and Truth* (1833) accounts for his rich public life as a celebrated man of letters and, most important, for the inner development of his poetic sensibility. The Japanese writer

Ryunosuke Akutagawa composed *A Fool's Life* (1927) in the months before his suicide as a final testament in the form of brief, intense reflections and experiences. With his *Experiment in Autobiography* (1934), the English novelist H. G. Wells both recounts his life story and conducts an inquiry into the future of fiction. *Speak, Memory* (1967) renders the exquisite patterns and ironies novelist Vladimir Nabokov has discovered in recollecting the first twenty years of his life, spent in his native Russia. Before he could write his retrospective autobiography *Aké: The Years of Childhood* (1981), which captures the wonders of early life experiences, the Nigerian poet and playwright Wole Soyinka was compelled to record *The Man Died: Prison Notes* (1972), a painful account of his survival as a political prisoner in the 1960s.

Literary art has also been achieved in autobiography by individuals from the other arts. The *Life* of Cellini, a sculptor and goldsmith, is the forerunner of compelling autobiographies by modern visual artists such as Marc Chagall's *Ma vie* (1931) and Man Ray's *Self-Portrait* (1963). In the musical arts, several autobiographies are noteworthy, ranging from *Chroniques de ma vie* (1935) by the modern European composer Igor Stravinksy to *Bound for Glory* (1943) by the American folk singer Woody Guthrie. A number of cinema's important directors—Sergei Eisenstein, Jean Renoir, Luis Buñuel, John Huston, and Akira Kurosawa—have written revealing accounts of their personal lives and their film art.

The art of autobiography is accomplished as well in many books by nonartists. The *Memoirs* (1796) by the historian Edward Gibbon and the *Autobiography* (1873) by the philosopher and social thinker John Stuart Mill forcefully recount the growth of mind and intellectual pursuits of these two prominent Englishmen. While prominence in established society was not afforded the American radical and journalist Agnes Smedley, her *Daughter of Earth* (1929) is a memorable record of personal history that, like Emma Goldman's *Living My Life* (1931), provides as well a political history of opposition to the ruling establishment.

Several modern spiritual autobiographies convey the search for faith and enlightenment with great eloquence. Mohandas Gandhi's *An Autobiography: The Story of My Experiments with Truth* (1929) depicts fulfillment of the individual soul through an ethical life in service to the political independence of India. For

Gandhi, spiritual realization comes through the development of a mass movement based on principles of *Satyagraha*, or "truth force." A different route to enlightenment is portrayed in Paramahansa Yogananda's *Autobiography of a Yogi* (1946), which recounts his progress toward self-mastery and his visionary experiences in both the Eastern and Western worlds. After the death of Simone Weil in 1943, her devotional reflections, mystical meditations, and an account of her own path to belief in Christ are gathered in the volume *Waiting for God* (1950). The poet Thomas Merton relates in *The Seven Storey Mountain* (1948) a search for identity and his spiritual renewal through Catholic devotion and the contemplative life.

The field of psychology has produced major works in the genre. Ironically, the *Autobiographical Study* (1925) written by Sigmund Freud is an unrevealing, strictly professional account of the external facts of his career. Freud's actual self-analysis through autobiography is conducted by degrees in his case studies of personal experience in works such as *The Interpretation of Dreams* (1900), *The Psychopathology of Everyday Life* (1901), and *Jokes and Their Relation to the Unconscious* (1905). An integral process of self-analysis is reached through autobiography in narrative form by Freud's student Theodor Reik and by Freud's rival in the science of mind, Carl Jung. Reik's *Listening with the Third Ear* (1948) is a professional autobiography as well, but the account of his case histories and interpersonal methods as a practicing analyst reveal the deep structure of his own mental processes. With *Memories, Dreams, Reflections* (1961) Jung, at age eighty-three, explores his "personal myth" and the manifestations of the collective unconscious in his personality.

In philosophy, the self and the first-person singular form of address have served as instruments of inquiry since René Descartes' *Discourse on Method* (1637) and its revolutionary declaration, "I think, therefore I am." The direct conversational tone in the *Discourse* is remarkable in a work of philosophy of the time, as is its personal account of Descartes' pursuit of knowledge. The possibilities for philosophy through the philosopher's self-examination are tested most passionately by Friedrich Nietzsche in *Ecce Homo: How One Becomes What One Is*, which was written in 1888 and first published in 1908. The title to the autobiography ("Behold the Man") is taken from the phrase with which Christ was sent to his martyrdom. The book promises nihilism instead of salvation, however, as the destiny of humanity. *Ecce Homo* is Nietzsche's last, exalted testament to his own iconoclastic principles and to ideas that resist order and reason.

The Italian philosopher and legal scholar Giambattista Vico wrote a narrative of his intellectual life in the period 1725–1731. Vico's *Autobiography*, as it was subsequently entitled, is composed in a third-person, historical mode in conscious reaction against the Cartesian method. A founder of modern historiography, Vico relies on narrative as the means to identify patterns of development and change in his intellectual growth. In Vico's book, history displaces speculative philosophy. Vico advanced a "new science" that adopts as its domain the world produced through human will and invention.

In the nineteenth century, the philosophical and theological inquiries of Søren Kierkegaard were directed toward the means by which individual consciousness and human truth emerge. In this line of inquiry, Kierkegaard concluded that subjective thinking and awareness of the paradoxical condition of individual existence are paths to the truths of human essence. John-Paul Sartre is one philosopher to have adapted these concepts of subjectivity, existence, and essence to the purposes of autobiography. In *Existentialism and Humanism* (1946), Sartre proposes that in forming an identity and a life the individual creates a purpose for humankind. His proposition that "existence precedes essence" means that humanity is defined by what individuals make of themselves. Sartre's *The Words* (1964), the subject of detailed discussion in a later chapter, is an ironic investigation in autobiography of the interplay between existence and essence.

Modern anthropology provides a wealth of views on matters of culture, language, social identity, and sexuality. Margaret Mead, an American anthropologist who has written extensively on patterns of personal development and differentiation in South Pacific island cultures, applies similar analysis to her own cultural evolution in the autobiography *Blackberry Winter* (1972). Claude Lévi-Strauss, a founder of structural anthropology, gives in *Tristes Tropiques* (1955) an account of his field work and interpretative methods. The search for meaning that Lévi-Strauss narrates in his autobiography leads to the fundamental proposition that myth and other features of culture function like a language system. In adopting this view of culture, Roland Barthes in his autobiography *Roland Barthes by Roland Barthes* (1975) replicates, through elaborate language play, the data, experiences, and recollections of his lifetime.

Masterworks in the genre place autobiography among the fundamental human sciences of anthropology, history, literature, philosophy, and psychology in its capacity to illuminate lived experience and social realities. As a historical and cultural projection of its democratic origins, moreover, autobiography has become of central importance in the contemporary assertion of social experience traditionally viewed as minority, marginal, or forbidden.

Autobiography possesses great appeal for mainstream culture, which is itself a result of the same democratic processes that nurtured the genre. Contemporary mass media and popular culture steadily reproduce mythic formulas of the success story, celebrity status, and the superstar in sports or entertainment, and autobiography serves the mass market as a cultural means of redistributing these formulas to consumers. The market value of an autobiography, however, does not prove to be a genuine measure of its cultural or social worth.

Beyond issues of its social and historical value, the literary potential of autobiography is most evident when the genre is evaluated as an art form. Autobiography can wholly immerse the reader in the experience and thought of another person. It can activate the reader to self-reflection and create a deep recognition of shared humanity. Autobiography is able to affect the reader in this manner because the experience it recounts can be at once unique and universal. The genre contributes directly to the wealth of shared experience that comprises human existence. The truths told in autobiography, as in much of imaginative literature, are not necessarily verifiable in objective, external reality or expressible as simple facts and ideas. Rather, the cultural value of autobiography is often subjective and internal. Its value is a matter of the heart and spirit as well as of the mind.

2

Franklin's *Autobiography* and the American Mythos of Success

A mong his many inventions, Benjamin Franklin created a prototype of individual enterprise before American capitalism had emerged in its now familiar form. Through his *Autobiography* Franklin has stood as the patron saint of success for businessmen across subsequent generations up through the present, from Sylvester Graham to P. T. Barnum, from Andrew Carnegie to Lee Iacocca. In these two centuries, American political economy has undergone extreme structural change, from the agrarian and handicraft stage of Franklin's colonial period to the monopoly capital industrialism of Carnegie's era and to our contemporary finance capital, postindustrial society.

Franklin's *Autobiography* is, among other things, a narrative of personal advancement in the commercial and political worlds of colonial North America. The *Autobiography* traces an implicit analogy between individual attainments and an emerging national history through the interrelation between personal experiences narrated within the book and public events that take place over the years during which Franklin writes his narrative.[1] The *Autobiography* is the original American success story. It charts the rise in individual fortunes of an individual American colonial from the perspective of a period during which American nationhood and prosperity are achieved. Franklin's life has become the paradigm for American lives ever since.

Franklin's *Autobiography* stands as an acknowledged paradigm for American success, as we shall see in the discussion of autobiographies by the entrepreneurs P. T. Barnum, Andrew Carnegie, and Lee Iacocca at the conclusion to this chapter. Franklin's principal means of success were his secular values, pragmatic aims, and self-promotion, which were all applied through the medium of prose in print. His principal measure of success was monetary reward and public recognition. Franklin was the first American to demonstrate that publication and publicity can be indispensable to the individual's social advancement. In doing so, Franklin redefined the Protestant sanctions of scripture and piety for American culture.

The composition of Part 1 to the *Autobiography* is dated 1771, during the time when Franklin was in England as an agent for four colonies. The political petitions and negotiations in which he was engaged would ultimately lead to separation from English rule. The events narrated in Part 1 cover the years 1706 to 1731 and end with Franklin's "first Project of a public Nature," the Subscription Library (Franklin, 57). The composition of Part 2 is dated 1784, a year that falls after the American Revolution and before the United States Constitution. In 1783 Franklin had concluded the negotiations for the peace pact with England that brought an end to the Revolutionary War. The events narrated in Part 2 extend from 1730 to 1733, the year of his project for the achievement of moral perfection.

Franklin worked on Parts 3 and 4 in the period 1788 to 1790, the year of his death. A member of the Constitutional Convention in 1787, Franklin was engaged in shaping the agreement over representation in the proposed Congress. The events narrated in the last two parts of the *Autobiography* extend from 1731 to 1760, starting with Franklin's idea in 1731 to form a Party of Virtue and the publication in 1732 of the first *Poor Richard's Almanack*. The unfinished *Autobiography* ends with Franklin in England, where he arrived in 1757 as a representative of Pennsylvania colony on matters of taxation, property ownership, and political representation.

The Mythos of the *Autobiography*

The personal history narrated within the *Autobiography*, which extends from 1706 to 1760, stands as a surrogate for the history of American independence and nationhood during the era in which Franklin wrote the book, 1771–1790. This pattern is a primary component of the mythos that posits Franklin's rise in individual fortunes as the archetype of American success. Generally, *mythos* is that pattern of meaning and values expressive of a culture's deep-rooted beliefs; the pattern is represented in symbolic fashion. In the thought of Aristotle, where the term is first applied to literary structure, mythos refers to the soul and shaping principle in an epic poem or a drama. In these genres, mythos is symbolized through the selection of events and their arrangement into a significant order. In tragedy, mythos is imitated through dramatic action and its formal structure is the play's plot. Aristotle's attention to mythos in literature concentrates on drama, where action has priority over character and thought (or, human motivation), drama's other primary components.

Northrop Frye has broadened the definitions of mythos to apply to all literary modes.[2] Frye treats mythos as a second order of imitation and representation. Mythos represents an action as typical and meaningful in a philosophical sense. The structure of events in narrative provides a dynamic rendering of the work's essential ideas. Mythos thus conveys thought through action. The patterns of typification and generalization detectable in human motivation contribute to the mythos of narrative. Frye further defines mythos in narrative as a structure of imagery in movement and as a design of intermediation between event and idea, example and precept.

When this critical perspective is directed toward the *Autobiography*, it becomes apparent that Franklin employs narrative to establish an interdependence between individual experience and universal truth. The mythos possible through narrative empowers Franklin to reconstruct an individual's original experiences, which inevitably include irregular and chance occurrences, into a rational human order founded on a reliable and beneficial causality. The logic with which his life story is imbued is a clear example of the alliance between discourse and narrative in autobiography. Through its narrative form, his *Autobiography* asserts the rationale of enterprise and worldly success, and the book still stands as a social mandate to the American individual.

Franklin composed Part 1 of the *Autobiography* in the form of a letter to his son William with the offer of his life story as exemplary: "Having emerg'd from the Poverty and Obscurity in which I was born and bred, to a State of Affluence and some Degree of Reputation in the World, and having gone so far thro' Life with a considerable Share of Felicity, the conducting Means I made use of, which with the Blessing of God, so well succeeded, my Posterity may like to know, as they may find some of them suitable to their own Situations, and therefore fit to be imitated" (Franklin, 1). Present-day readers might naturally assume that Franklin's son is at the time of the letter a young man starting out in the world, but in 1771 William Franklin was forty years old and held the powerful position of Royal Governor of New Jersey. Through the form of a personal letter of advice, Franklin attempts to maintain some paternal influence over his son, who would remain loyal to British rule through the 1770s.[3] More broadly, Benjamin Franklin's letter in effect addressed American posterity and, in yet another instance of public service, it proposes his means of social advancement as instruments fit to be imitated.

Franklin's principal instrument of advancement had been his skill in the language arts. His mastery of prose-writing came initially through methodical imitation. The practical arts of writing and printing provide the *Autobiography*, a model of utilitarian prose, with its most expansive metaphors. Franklin's father intended a church career for Benjamin. A pious uncle (after whom the family had named Benjamin) provided the boy with numerous volumes of sermons that this uncle had recorded in a shorthand script of his own invention. Uncle Benjamin had instructed the boy in decoding this shorthand, but Franklin did not practice the writing system and thus did not retain it. In narrating his advancement *away* from training for a church career at this formative point in life, Franklin supposes that the uncle provided the sermons "as a Stock to set up with, if I would learn his Character" (Franklin, 6). The immediate reference in this phrase is to the system of shorthand, while the figurative reference is clearly to the uncle's personality trait of piety, a quality that

Franklin hereby indicates he was disinclined to imitate or thus acquire at that age.

Sent to Grammar School at age eight, Franklin spent no more than a year there. His father soon determined that advanced academic training was too expensive for the family and that it could well lead anyway to "the mean Living many so educated were afterwards able to obtain" (Franklin, 6). Franklin's second and last year of formal education was at a Boston school for writing and arithmetic where he quickly acquired a skill at "fair Writing" (that is, a legible handwritten script) but made no progress at arithmetic (Franklin, 6). Seven years later, Franklin applied himself to the study of a standard arithmetic text and thus acquired competency in basic mathematics. Within the *Autobiography*, Franklin's narrative incorporates forms of moral stockkeeping and business accounting.

The principal phase of Franklin's self-education after his short-lived formal schooling was his acquisition of a useful prose style. Though the apprenticeship as a printer to his brother John had enabled him to attain correct and regular mechanics in his writing by the time he became a teenager, the manner and method of his prose expression remained undeveloped. With the purchase of a volume that reprinted Joseph Addison and Richard Steele's daily paper the *Spectator* (published originally in 1711–1712 and 1714), Franklin began a systematic imitation of its prose style, posing himself the assignment of essaying the same topics as he found in the newspaper. Upon comparison of his efforts with the original articles, Franklin attentively set about identifying, correcting, and amending the "Faults" in his prose (Franklin, 12). Minor signs of his improvements upon the originals, Franklin indicates, "encourag'd me to think I might possibly in time come to be a tolerable English Writer, of which I was extremely ambitious" (Franklin, 12).

The next phase of self-education entailed development of an effective rhetorical manner. Upon encountering examples of the Socratic method, Franklin was greatly attracted to its strategies as an alternative to "a Positive assuming Manner that seldom fails to disgust [and] tends to create Opposition" (Franklin, 14). With telling frequency, Franklin confesses in the *Autobiography* that by inclination he was as a young man abrupt, assertive, disputatious, and satiric. But he quickly recognized the advantages of indirection, modesty, discretion, and humble doubt in public discourse. The circumstances behind the first publication of Franklin's writings exemplify their effectiveness.

Franklin as Writer and Publisher

In 1722, at age sixteen, Franklin had advanced through stages of imitation to a preliminary stage of invention in his writing. In listening to conversations among the contributors to his brother's paper the *New England Courant*, Franklin was excited by the success brought by their "writing little Pieces for this Paper, which gain'd it Credit, and made it more in Demand" (Franklin, 15). With the expectation of interference borne of jealousy from his brother James, to whom he was apprenticed, Franklin masked the handwriting of his first contribution.

In the form of a letter signed "Silence Dogood," Franklin submitted his composition to the printing house after business hours. Franklin continued in this guise for six months until he had expended his fund of ideas in fourteen Dogood submissions. It is a compelling fact that Franklin's first success in prose was thus achieved through indirection, keys to which were the disguised "character" of his handwritten script and the assumption of an unpretentious, feminine personality in Silence Dogood.

As anticipated, when Franklin revealed his identity as the Silence Dogood author, James Franklin grew hostile and tyrannical in the treatment of his young brother and apprentice. Benjamin Franklin had learned how to read the character of his older brother. In time, Franklin developed great skills in what can be termed "social literacy"—that is, his ready comprehension of each personality among the varied host of individuals with whom he came in contact. There are notable errors in his early reading of character, however, as in the case of his trust in Governor William Keith, whose false promises left Franklin stranded in London in 1724. The *Autobiography* is rich in the study of personalities, including Franklin's own.

The terms of his apprenticeship to James Franklin were stringent, particularly when one considers that they were drawn between immediate family members. Where a normal apprenticeship indentured a person for seven years, Benjamin Franklin was apprenticed to his brother for a term of nine years. But printing and publication were unexpectedly to provide him a means of emancipation from his indenture.

His brother was jailed for nearly a month in 1722, after the *Courant*'s publication of an article deemed a libel against British authority. The condition of his release stipulated that James Franklin was prohibited from publishing the *Courant*. To circumvent this regulation, James Franklin decided to create the appearance of Benjamin's independence from the apprenticeship and have the newspaper published under his younger brother's name. A discharge from indenture was written on the original documents, but James contracted a private indenture with Benjamin for the full original term and he retained this contract secretly.

Within months, another disagreement between the brothers prompted Franklin to break his indenture, confident that James would not make the secret contract public. Franklin succeeded in gaining his independence in this manner. His action was expedient, but the *Autobiography* calculates it to have been a dishonest ploy: "It was not fair in me to take this Advantage, and this I therefore reckon one of the first Errata of my Life" (Franklin, 16–17). *Errata* is the copyediting and printing term that designates unintentional errors. Used in place of *offense* or *wrong* in such contexts, this neutral term relieves Franklin from a degree of responsibility and guilt.

Errata are readily correctable errors, as Franklin shrewdly indicates in the opening statement to his *Autobiography*: "I should have no Objection to a Repetition of the same Life from its Beginning, only asking the Advantage Authors have in a second Edition to correct some Faults of the first" (Franklin, 1). To correct is not the same as to repent or to make restitution. By clear implication, this statement displaces God from the position of author of Franklin's life and offers the *Autobiography* itself as second edition to the original life Franklin self-authored. Providence is credited only with a role in guiding Franklin to the models and instruments he adopted in turning experience to his best advantage.

In its progression as a secular success story, the *Autobiography* more than compensates for acknowledged personal faults by offering accounts of exemplary actions. After violation of the indentures and his brother's obstruction of any employment as a printer in Boston, Franklin sets out at age seventeen to seek his fortune. From this point forward he undertakes to make his own destiny, which dawns with his famous entry into Philadelphia. That humorous self-portrait of his "awkward ridiculous Appearance"—munching a puffy roll with two more held under his arms, his coat pockets bulging with the extra traveling clothes stuffed into them—marks the archetypal humble beginnings in a modern bourgeois success story (Franklin, 20).[4]

Aptly metaphoric is the fact that the main thoroughfare down which he first walks is named Market Street. Within a few years, as his printing and stationery businesses in the city prosper, Franklin will advertise his diligence by pushing a wheelbarrow with new paper stock down the same Philadelphia streets. Franklin's entry into Philadelphia serves as the measuring point equally for society's advancement and for his own success. The *Autobiography* offers evidence of the city's economic progress and of his own by 1729 through a comparison with the depressed conditions of both at the time of his arrival in 1723. This direct correlation between the public good and the personal career forms the mythos to his book.

Another erratum Franklin acknowledges is the indulgence of his sexual urges as a young man. The *Autobiography* discloses this information at the close of Part 1 not for purposes of sensationalism but as a cautionary example of "Expense and great Inconvenience, besides a continual Risk to . . . Health by a Distemper" (Franklin, 56). In the same period of Franklin's life and through just such a liaison, his illegitimate son William was conceived. Though Part 1 is addressed to William, the *Autobiography* never broaches this delicate issue. The book does not do so because in Franklin's view the intimate matter is of no public utility beyond the categorical caution he states. The erratum of sexual license is corrected narratively by Part 1's concluding depiction of Franklin's initial action as a public benefactor, establishment of the first subscription library.

Character in the *Autobiography*

The autobiography thus advances the life story as a success story through such emendations and progressions in the narrative order. The errata Franklin enumerates in the *Autobiography* constituted, when they occurred originally, impediments to the useful development of personality. The manner in which Franklin represents them in his narrative is indicative of his principles of social accountability. The *Autobiography* is extensively descriptive of his *character*, as in the account of how, as a young printer, he was careful to maintain the appearance of industry. Beyond the memorable tableau of his youthful entry into Philadelphia, however, the book provides little information on Franklin's physical appearance.

Franklin applies the term *character* to many purposes. In relation to writing, it refers to the individuality, regularity, and system of one's orthography. In the printing trade, it refers to the set of preformed letters and the style of typography. In a letter written at the time he undertook Part 2 of the *Autobiography*, Franklin draws a political analogy from this context to praise the American character type: "I, as a Republican Printer, always like a Form well *plain'd down*; being averse to those *overbearing* Letters that hold their Heads so *high*, as to hinder their Neighbours from appearing."[5]

In an *Almanack* entry for 1750 Franklin comments on the cultural value of writing: "What an admirable Invention is Writing, by which a Man may communicate his Mind without opening his Mouth. . . . 'Tis a Pity this excellent Art has not preserved the Name and Memory of its Inventor" (*Writings*, 1259). Jean-Jacques Rousseau, his contemporary, considered language to have evolved from human passions and its first forms to have been poetic. Characteristically, Franklin's interest in language is pragmatic, as demonstrated in his speculation that its written form is the product of individual invention.

In reference to personality, Franklin commonly uses *character* in an active sense in connection with the methods by which an individual can accumulate and practice useful traits. The distinguishing traits of greatest value to an individual are not inherent ones but are rather qualities acquired through learning and imitation, as in his famous program for moral perfection. The *Autobiography* compares that program to the process of practice at copybooks for the purpose of developing "fair and legible" handwriting (Franklin, 73). For the purposes of Franklin's colonial enterprises, character was his start-up capital. Indebted to the model of prudence, sound judgment, and public spirit in men like his father, Franklin states, "I had therefore a tolerable Character to begin the World with, I valued it properly, and determin'd to preserve it" (Franklin, 46).

The return on the individual's deliberate and public development of character is social and economic credit. The elder autobiographer savors the ironies of his youthful ambitions to perfect his character. With a thrust of social satire, he concludes that a spotless character would ultimately have brought discredit upon him among business colleagues and politicians. The connections between *character* and *credit*, however, are everywhere else affirmed in the *Autobiography*. In the social sphere, character is the acknowledged value of one's public life. By extension, it refers to the description or report of a person's qualities—to a character reference.

In describing his serious courtship of a Philadelphia woman who belonged to a family of some means, the *Autobiography* gives an unsentimental account of its failure in 1729 or 1730. As the two discussed future plans, Franklin set the condition that her family pay off his remaining debts for the printing-house, which amounted to about 100 pounds. When her family responded that they did not have this sum available, he advised that they mortgage their house. They refused and voiced doubts about his reputation and his prospects for success in the printing business. Deeply offended by any reservations about his credit and his character, Franklin broke off all relations with the woman and her family.

The personal letters to Franklin that stand as preface to Part 2 of the *Autobiography* serve as *bona fides* for the civic and commercial value of his life story. They present a set of complementary rationales for the continuation and publication of the narrative. A record of Franklin's life of temperance and industry, these letters reason, promises to serve as a useful and instructive example to promote these virtues. That record also constitutes an advertisement for the opportunities and advantages of life in the new country. Continuation of the life story also would provide an occasion to publish a discourse that in the 1730s Franklin had planned to write under the title *The Art of Virtue*. Though the discourse was never written, in 1784 Franklin reconstitutes its essential ideas for Part 2 of the *Autobiography*.

One additional rationale offered in the prefatory letters is that the autobiography would protect Franklin's exemplary life from the depredations of unauthorized biographies. This preemptive rationale is one that Henry Adams later adopted in deciding to write and publish privately his autobiography, *The Education of Henry Adams* (1907; 1918). In this case, the rationale is suggested in order to persuade Franklin to secure and fix a likeness for his own character. During his residence in France in the 1780s, Franklin encountered his physical likeness duplicated in numerous pictures, busts, and prints. As Leo Braudy has remarked, this cultural phenomenon expressed a new objectification of identity, at once "venerated and trivialized."[6] In a portrait of this American in Paris, Herman Melville characterizes Franklin as "the type and genius of his land [who was] everything but a poet."[7]

While Franklin does not deploy his character to poetic ends, he does employ it toward mythic ends in his narrative of a tradesman's economic and civic progress. Good character increases the value of personality as a social asset, putting the individual in a higher position of trust in business and political matters. It enhances the individual's exchange and investment values. A reputation for integrity and reliability is social capital. As Max Weber explained, Franklin's differentiation between the *appearance* of a virtue like humility and its *actuality* in a man's social life is not unethical or hypocritical; rather it is a pragmatic recognition of the secular currency of Protestant values.[8]

It is for the maintenance of a creditable account of character that the *Autobiography* assesses a limited number of Franklin's own imperfections and errata. The narrative dispenses strong criticism over the disreputable personal habits and business practices of many fellow colonials Franklin encountered in his career. But it rarely pursues the suggestions of fast dealing and sharp practices in Franklin's own business affairs, suggestions that lie occasionally at the margins of his narrative. Self-scrutiny over such matters would impede the narrative's momentum as a mythos of success and depress the value of character as social currency.

The *Autobiography* records the political debate and negotiations at the end of the 1720s over the matter of a new issue of paper money in the Pennsylvania and Delaware colonies. As a proponent of increased monetary supply and circulation, Franklin wrote and published the pamphlet *The Nature and Necessity of a Paper Currency* in 1729. The tract appeared anonymously, but members of the legislature knew the identity of its author, and after the measure passed they commissioned subsequent printing contracts to Franklin's business. While admitting the pamphlet "had been of some Service," Franklin sees no collusion in these events and interprets the award of printing contracts to him as "another Advantage gain'd by my being able to write" (Franklin, 53). Franklin had indeed recognized the value of the printing trades.

Another incident recounted in the *Autobiography* reflects on Franklin's writing and publishing enterprises. In 1734 the Presbyterian preacher Samuel Hemphill arrived in the colony from Ireland, and he attracted a sizable if short-lived following with the eloquence of his sermons. Though opponents revealed that Hemphill had completely plagiarized these sermons, Franklin continued to support him for the following reason: "I rather approv'd his giving us good Sermons compos'd by others, than bad ones of his own Manufacture" (Franklin, 82). Franklin leaves unexplored, however, the liberal literary borrowing conducted in his *Almanacks* and newspapers in this period. Any suspicion by the reader of impropriety in such regards is outweighed by the narrative's certification of Franklin's civic services, as in his donation of the stove design to the public domain by declining to register a patent for it.

Pragmatism and Moral Principles

By Franklin's business standards—if not always by his business practices—vanity and ostentation are unproductive. The *Autobiography* opens, however, with an ironic admission that an unmodified degree of vanity lies at the foundation of his personality. Franklin makes the admission with the recognition that in writing an autobiography the appearance of self-absorption is an occupational hazard. In the program for moral perfection, Franklin places Humility thirteenth and last on the table of virtues: "Imitate Jesus and Socrates," a decidedly prideful ambition (Franklin, 68). Immediately prior to presenting that program in Part 2, Franklin argues on behalf of the utility of vanity, a vanity controlled and disguised in order for the individual to escape envy and to benefit the community. Ever the ironist, Franklin admits to pride over the degree of humility he has been able to achieve. His estimation of vanity's relative harmfulness and usefulness is a sign of how secularized and situational his values are, for in a Puritan context this character quality directly opens the matter of cardinal sin.

An instance of economic vanity, in the form of conspicuous consumption, is contained in Part 1. Upon a visit to Boston after his successful first year in Philadelphia, Franklin returned to the printing house owned by his brother James. Dressed for the occasion in genteel fashion, Franklin displayed to the journeymen a handful of silver currency and a pocket watch. He also gave them a piece of eight to spend in the barroom. Franklin acknowledges that his "Raree-Show" infuriated his estranged brother John, but he pleads, unpersuasively perhaps, that he had not meant to provoke envy or to humiliate his brother in front of the workmen (Franklin, 24).

There was in Franklin distinct traits of the showman and promoter, and in this he is a precursor to P. T. Barnum. While in London in the period 1724 to 1726, he traded in American curiosities. Among the items in his possession was a purse made of asbestos, which, the *Autobiography* claims, was such a rarity that an English collector sought out Franklin and purchased it. In fact, Franklin had solicited and initiated the meeting with this collector. Franklin also ventured to demonstrate his own prowess at swimming to an audience of traveling companions by jumping into the Thames. One of these companions was so captivated by Franklin's abilities that he suggested they form an exhibition tour for Europe. In the 1740s he drafted two lectures for Ebenezer Kinnersley to use in a demonstration on Franklin's theories of electricity before paying audiences. These business ventures in public performance reflect another meaning of *character* for Franklin: the exhibition of one's advertised abilities and knowledge.

The most widely circulated promotional piece by Franklin in his era was the tract that came to be known as "The Way to Wealth," first published in 1758 and reissued over 140 times before 1800. As in the previous personae of Silence Dogood and Poor Richard Saunders, the tract's Father Abraham is a humble, worldly, and pragmatic soul. The occasion of Father Abraham's homily is the hour prior to a public auction, for which a large crowd has gathered. With Franklin's customary irony, this setting hints at Vanity Fair in John Bunyan's Puritan narrative *Pilgrim's Progress* (Part 1, 1678; Part 2, 1684). Like Bunyan, Franklin locates worldly snares at the auction ground, but they are impediments to the progress of business, not to that of the soul. Father Abraham's text is *Poor Richard's Almanack* rather than Scripture: "Trusting too much to others Care is the Ruin of many; for, as the *Almanack* says, *In the Affairs of this World, Men are saved, not by Faith, but by the Want of it*" (*Writings*, 1298). That is to say, faith is incompatible with the prudence and scrutiny necessary in business affairs. The venerable Abraham advances the premise that wealth is the way to virtue, a view later echoed by Irish playwright George Bernard Shaw.

As the *Autobiography* explains, early in adulthood Franklin developed the practice of dedicating Sunday to useful studies. His program for moral perfection took the form of a tradesman's devotional book. Alongside the wisdom of Solomon it contained inscriptions from Cicero, Addison, and the poet James Thomson. It was at the same time a life-planner and a day-planner with its "Scheme of Employment for the Twenty-four Hours of a Natural Day" (Franklin, 71). Underlying its proscriptions against idleness, pride, and errancy is the simple calculation that such failings tax man by their cost to him in reputation and income.

Utility and pragmatism are the first principles of Franklin's mature beliefs. The *Autobiography* provides a comic instance in recounting how reason overcame ethical doctrine when the scent of frying cod led Franklin to break his rule against eating animal food. By logical deduction he reasoned that this fish fed on other species of fish, and thus, in turn, he was justified in feeding on it. On the basis of this resourceful rationalization of an appetitive urge, Franklin draws the conclusion: "So convenient a thing it is to be a *reasonable Creature*, since it enables one to find or make a Reason for everything one has a mind to do" (Franklin, 28). In making this generalization, Franklin asserts the faculty of mind where his example emphasizes the digestive organs, a substitution characteristic of his habits of thought. Franklin, like many entrepreneurs since him, had an appetite and an instinct for the main chance.

Franklin's vegetarian diet and abstinence from intoxicants served equally as an experiment in ethical principles and as a practical method of saving money. His first adult intellectual inclinations had been toward necessitarianism and deism. But with the recognition that such forms of freethinking were often accompanied by a loss to one's social reputation, Franklin reached the pragmatic conclusion that though they may be true, these doctrines are not ultimately useful. In developing his mature beliefs Franklin effectively rationalized and secularized the Protestant practices of moral self-examination. The *Autobiography* lends Franklin's life to the system of rational bookkeeping that was instrumental in the rise of capitalism.

The mythos underlying narrative in the *Autobiography* proposes that Franklin's success is by equal measures that of a tradesman and that of a philosopher. Through authorial masks like The Busy-Body and Richard Saunders, his early writing for the press markets a homespun philosophy. Among the last endeavors narrated in the *Autobiography* are technical and scientific investigations (in areas like electricity and ship design) that belong to the branch of science he terms, in the nomenclature of the era, "experimental Philosophy" (Franklin, 133). Printing plays a primary role here as well. It is through the publication and translation of his reports on electricity that Franklin's theory gained credibility. And the *Autobiography* leaves to posterity the project of determining the most efficient ship design. Franklin figuratively commissions the determination of the necessary dimensions for hull and masts and of the best method of rigging: "This is the Age of Experiments; and such a Set accurately made and combined would be of great Use. I am therefore persuaded that ere long some ingenious Philosopher will undertake it—to whom I wish Success" (Franklin, 141).

Franklin's greatest, most enduring experiment was of course himself. The *Autobiography* narrates his life as a progressive assumption of new social roles, of new occupations, and, perhaps most famously, of new character traits. Franklin developed character traits, and made them habitual, for the purpose of advancement in society and business. The thirteen virtues in his program for moral perfection all serve the individual's reputation and public worth. A majority of them—temperance, silence, order, resolution, frugality, industry, and moderation—function as well on behalf of the work ethic and of emerging capitalist practices.

Franklin availed himself of opportunity in the New World largely through the instrument of writing. His life's work was regularly pursued through squibs, letters, reports, editorials, almanacs, scientific papers, promotional pieces, pamphlets, notices, contracts, and government documents. Robert Sayre has observed of such activity that "the printed page was obviously the medium through which he learned many of the gestures and postures of his multiple lives."[9] For this complete man of letters, the printing press revolutionized the means of production and of self-reproduction. The pattern of success traced in the *Auto-biography* leads from reading to writing, and from writing to printing. In printing, he progressed from newspapers to tracts, then to government commissions for documents and paper currency.

The best-selling Franklin prose during his era is composed of a proverbial language of economic self-interest. In identifying the origins of such thought and expression, the *Autobiography* quotes the frequent counsel given to Franklin as a boy by his father, who extracted it from the Proverbs of Solomon: "*Seest thou a Man diligent in his Calling, he shall stand before Kings, he shall not stand before mean Men*" (Franklin, 64). This citation of Proverbs 22:29 in the *Autobiography* substitutes *Calling* where the word in both the Geneva Bible and the King James Version—the two principal translations read in New England at the time—is *business*.[10] The transposition signals an intriguing, inverted illustration of Max Weber's general thesis about Franklin's exemplary role in the secularization of religious values. In substituting the commonly religious term for a normally secular one, Franklin here confers moral authority and divine sanction on worldly endeavors.

Franklin's creed is not so much a gospel of wealth as it is a gospel of rationalized work, whose reward is wealth. As Weber has explained, Franklin is just one prominent practitioner in the general social movement that redefined "calling" (the summoning by God) to mean the positive, ethical value of routine activity in the secular world and the fulfillment of duties and obligations in commercial transactions. With pride, the *Autobiography* reports that "The Way to Wealth" was translated and widely distributed in Europe, even by members of the clergy to their poor parishioners. It also reports that at home, in the colony of Pennsylvania, many believed the tract "had its share of Influence in producing that growing Plenty of Money which was observable for several Years after its Publication" (Franklin, 79).

The American Success Story in Autobiography

P. T. Barnum cites Franklin in his popular lecture "The Art of Money Getting" among a diverse host of authorities on the subject that also includes Shakespeare, the Rothschilds, and Davy Crockett. The Barnum lecture, first given in London on 29 December 1858, promotes secular values to advance commercial ends for an emerging industrial society and its unprecedented democracy of leisure and consumption.[11] On tour in England during 1859, Barnum delivered the lecture nearly 100 times.

"The Art of Money Getting" has an unexpected echo in the views of Ralph Waldo Emerson, whose essay "Wealth" was first published in 1860. Where Barnum asserts that the money-getter is the benefactor of humanity and that commercial enterprise writes the history of civilization, Emerson proposes that money is representative: "The counting-room maxims liberally expounded are laws of the universe. The merchant's economy is a coarse symbol of the soul's economy."[12] For Emerson, the commercial and philosophical values of speculation are ultimately compatible.

Rather than the neat ironies, utilitarian prose, and aphorisms of Franklin's *Autobiography*, Barnum's autobiographies are full of rhetorical flourishes, superlatives, and absolute statements. First published in 1855, Barnum's autobiography was expanded in

two later editions (1869 and 1889) to capitalize upon new generations of audiences.[13] In relating the triumph of many show
attractions over the years, Barnum repeatedly claims in his narrative that each new sensation drew public interest "unheard of"
and "never before equalled." The fundamental economic principles Barnum codifies in "The Art of Money Getting" are ones of
speculation and expenditure and are a departure from the rules
of prudence and thrift it cites on the authority of Franklin. The
mythos propounded through the autobiographies and the lecture indicates that in enterprises like Barnum's often it is not
moderation but rather lavish expense that begets more money.

Ostentation and buying at a high price can serve as further
forms of advertising. Barnum's firmest commercial conviction is
in the power of advertising. For him, advertising is a medium
that demonstrates the profitability of excess. In the autobiography of his New York City boyhood in the 1850s, novelist Henry
James recalls the vivid impression made by the abundance of
posters and performance placards along Fifth Avenue advertising Barnum's American Museum: "These announcements . . .
engaged my attention, whenever I passed, as the canvas of a
great master in a great gallery holds that of the pious tourist."[14]

Another nineteenth-century entrepreneur to invoke the
authority of Franklin is the industrialist Andrew Carnegie,
whose autobiography quotes Franklin's axiom "the highest worship of God is service to man" as the rationale underlying
Carnegie's philanthropic endeavors. The Protestant ethic reaches
a pinnacle of secular piety in Carnegie's essay "The Gospel of
Wealth," a title given it by a journal editor upon its publication
in 1889 and that Carnegie adopts as a chapter title in his
Autobiography.

The principal tenets to "The Gospel of Wealth" reflect the beneficial social Darwinism and the confidence in inevitable
progress that Carnegie gained through his adherence to the
thought of the social philosopher Herbert Spencer. The individual's instinct for profit is the prime mover in capitalist society's
process of natural selection. Virtue functions for the individual as
a matter of just calculation and deliberation of the greatest
self-interest. Property, wealth, and the management of industry
are, in such a context, sacred trusts by the means of which an
entrepreneur governs the advancement of civilization.

The first penny Andrew Carnegie earned outside the family circle is an event remarkable enough to be narrated in his *Autobiography*. In his youthful employments Carnegie progressed from bobbin-boy and boiler attendant to messenger. The *Autobiography* describes his first raise in wages at the Pittsburgh telegraph office as an event that brought tears of joy to his parents and spiritual fulfillment to himself: "Here was heaven upon earth."[15] Monetary accumulation also brought Carnegie an aesthetic sense of ecstasy. When he started work as a manager in the railroads, he drew his salary in gold pieces: "They seemed to me the prettiest works of art in the world" (*Carnegie*, 77). It is a point of pride for Carnegie that his success came as a manufacturer and not as a speculator, a financial class whom he disdains as "a parasite feeding upon values, creating none" (*Carnegie*, 154).

Like Carnegie, the automobile manufacturer Lee Iacocca asserts personal integrity in his autobiography through a mythos of individual prowess in the American arena of industrial production and competition. The principal adversary for the heroic industrialist in this struggle to preserve integrity is finance capitalism and speculative investment. Iacocca traces the origins of this mythos directly to the values of his father, who "constantly preached his gospel of fiscal responsibility."[16] Iacocca names Benjamin Franklin, in the company of other Americans like Joe DiMaggio and Harry Truman, as a lifelong personal cultural hero. But the vision required to direct a modern manufacturing enterprise cannot simply rely on a tradesman's economic principles. Iacocca disdains the mentality of the "bean counters" in the executive and administrative offices of Ford Motor Company during his presidency there.

In recounting the success of Ford Motor Company under his management, Iacocca makes a claim equivalent to one of paternity for its most profitable products: "The Mustang, the Mark III, and the Fiesta were my babies" (*Iacocca*, 120). Deposed as a captain of industry by Henry Ford II in 1978, Iacocca took over at the failing Chrysler Corporation, and he became more of a crisis manager than a manufacturer for the first two years there. On behalf of a make-over of the Chrysler corporate image, Iacocca accepted a proposal from the company's advertising agency that he be featured in a media campaign to restore the public's confidence in Chrysler automobiles. The autobiography describes this endorsement technique as a means of establishing credibility for the advertising claims of value, reliability, and economy. The commercial campaign also satisfied Iacocca's need for a paternal identity in relation to the manufactured products.

As did Carnegie in his era, Iacocca laments the shift from industry to finance in American enterprise: "From a nation whose strength has always flowed from investments in the production and consumption of goods, we have somehow turned into a nation enamored with investing in paper" (*Iacocca*, 327). But the preservation of Chrysler Corporation required a financial deal with the U.S. Government at a scale and in a manner unprecedented in American business history, through a Federal guaranteed loan of $1.2 billion. In recounting these events, the autobiography acknowledges the magnitude of this violation of his father's principles of fiscal prudence, but Iacocca was engaged in his own higher, paternal mission to spare the corporation from bankruptcy. Iacocca presided over the symbolic rebirth of Chrysler when he presented the government with a major loan repayment in 1983, seven years ahead of the debt schedule.

Readers may doubt that the lives of Benjamin Franklin, P. T. Barnum, Andrew Carnegie, and Lee Iacocca were in fact as consistently successful or as tirelessly dedicated as their autobiographies make these lives seem. Irrespective of such doubts, however, their autobiographies remain true to the mythic American significance of the enterprising individual's material success and public influence.

3

Narrative of the Life of Frederick Douglass, an American Slave

Literacy and Liberation in African-American Autobiography

The social and literary power of many African-American auto-biographies is rooted in a compelling relationship between literacy and liberation in the life of the autobiographer and in the telling of that life. Both within the era of slavery and over the 100 years of segregation after the Emancipation Proclamation (1863), individual African-Americans deployed autobiography to obtain a degree of social and cultural enfranchisement before their people had gained basic political and human rights.

Correlations between literacy and liberation in African-American culture have been widely explored. In an examination of the "pregeneric" phase of African-American writing—that is, the shared narratives and myths that shape its literary forms—Robert Stepto discovers that "the primary pregeneric myth for Afro-America is the quest for freedom and literacy."[1] The slave narrative documents and authenticates, through literate form, this quest for freedom, and it thus established autobiography as a genre central to African-American literature. Commenting on the process of political and cultural legitimization for the African-American self, Henry Louis Gates, Jr., explains that "to become subjects . . . black ex-slaves had to demonstrate their language-using capacity before they could become social and historical entities."[2] The juncture of literacy with the struggle for freedom in personal narratives by ex-slaves such as Frederick Douglass, Harriet Jacobs, and William Wells Brown marks a mythic source, drawn upon by many subsequent African–American narratives, in both fiction and autobiography.

Since literacy is a matter of much debate in contemporary American culture and education, its meanings in the present critical context should be clarified. E. D. Hirsch, Jr., defines the standard of "cultural literacy" for American society as the background information that a reader possesses and that makes possible the reader's comprehension of the daily newspaper. His admittedly conservative definition does not consider any issues of literate Americans' ability to question the truth of what they read. Though he concedes that "the superficiality of the knowledge we need for reading and writing may be unwelcome news to those who deplore superficial learning and praise critical thinking over mere information," Hirsch defends a standard of literacy based in unquestioning mental responses.[3] Hirsch has gone on to promote this superficiality and to trade on cultural literacy as a consumer product with the publication of *The Dictionary of Cultural Literacy*.[4]

Educators like Paulo Freire and Ivan Illich, however, define literacy as a cognitive power with the potential for social liberation. Freire has engaged in adult literacy campaigns in peasant societies and urban slums as a form of cultural politics. Basic education in reading and writing has a potential to empower individuals disenfranchised by class, race, or geography. Thus Freire values literacy as an instrument for critical consciousness, for political emancipation, and ultimately for social and historical transformation: "Reading the world always precedes reading the word, and reading the word implies continually reading the world. . . . Reading the word is not preceded merely by reading the world, but by a certain form of *writing* it or *rewriting* it, that is, of transforming it by means of conscious, practical work."[5] This kind of literacy obviously goes well beyond a surface ability to read and write and should be understood as "social literacy," an aspect of which we have already encountered in Franklin's *Autobiography*. For Franklin it meant an ability to read the motives and self-interest of the individuals with whom he engaged in business and politics. Nate Shaw, in his autobiography *All God's Dangers* (1974), articulates great social knowledge though segregation in the American South, and lifelong labor in the fields, had deprived him of a formal education.

Speech acts—whether they be reading, writing, or simply conversation—have a potential to generate social power. For Frederick Douglass, the expression of individual identity is inseparable from protest over the shared fate of African–Americans under the institutions of slavery and racism. The full title of Douglass's first autobiography is *Narrative of the Life of Frederick Douglass, an American Slave, Written by Himself* (1845). The epithet "an American Slave" accents a fundamental contradiction between American political ideals and American social reality. The title phrase "Written by Himself" is one *bona fide* that the narrative was not a ghost written or fictionalized account by a white author, an allegation regularly brought against such books by defenders of slavery. Similarly, a preface by William Lloyd Garrison and a letter from Wendell Phillips, two prominent white New England abolitionists, precede the Douglass narrative as guarantees of its authenticity. The verified existence of an intelligent, compassionate, and articulate voice like Douglass's testifies to the complete humanity of the slave, a quality denied in the ideology of slaveholders.

The Life and Writings of Douglass

In his twenties when he wrote the *Narrative*, Frederick Douglass published two other autobiographies over the course of his distinguished life: *My Bondage and My Freedom* in 1855 and *Life and Times of Frederick Douglass* in 1881, with a revised edition issued in 1892, three years before his death. In addition to updating his life history, the successive autobiographies incorporate, reshape, and unfold material from the *Narrative*. They revise many initial memories and responses, as in the matter of the transitory contact with his mother and the troubling issue of being fathered by a white man, who was probably his first owner. The account of

Douglass's escape from slavery is detailed only in *Life and Times*. He withheld from the two antebellum autobiographies (the *Narrative* and *My Bondage and My Freedom*) the particulars of his planned flight for fear that any such disclosure might jeopardize similar escape efforts by other slaves.

While the evolution of Douglass's life story across these three books comprises a fascinating study in autobiography, the focus here is on his first account of liberation.[6] In 1838 Douglass escaped from Baltimore, where he had worked as a craftsman in the shipbuilding trade, though the wages he earned were turned over to his master. That same year Douglass married Anna Murray, a freewoman, and they settled in New Bedford, Massachusetts, where he could find employment only as a common laborer. Douglass became active in the city's African Methodist Episcopal Zion church, and in 1839 he began to speak against slavery to the congregation. On 11 August 1841 Douglass was for the first time a featured speaker before a white audience, at an antislavery convention in Nantucket. This event is the last one recounted in the *Narrative*, and it prompts him to reflect: "It was a severe cross, and I took it up reluctantly. The truth was, I felt myself a slave, and the idea of speaking to white people weighed me down. I spoke but a few moments, when I felt a degree of freedom, and said what I desired with considerable ease. From that time until now, I have been engaged in pleading the cause of my brethren—with what success, and with what devotion, I leave those acquainted with my labors to decide."[7]

At the time the *Narrative* was published, by the Anti-Slavery Office in Boston, Douglass remained a slave by the legal terms of the federal Fugitive Slave Act. Having revealed his present location in the *Narrative* and still liable to capture and return South, in 1845 Douglass left the United States for England, where he lectured against slavery for nearly two years. While in England, supporters initiated a campaign to buy his freedom, which was completed in 1846 with the purchase of Frederick Douglass from his master Thomas Auld and the registration of Douglass's free papers in Baltimore. Douglass never lost sight of the brutal irony that his free papers were legitimized through a bill of sale.

Years prior to this individual, contractual release from slavery, Douglass initiated a process of social emancipation through his speeches at abolitionist meetings. Before that, from adolescence onward, he had already initiated a process of psychological emancipation while in the South. To that psychological emancipation—marked by his resolve at age fifteen not to be beaten again—he added the command of language. Indeed, Douglass emerged as one of the foremost American orators of the nineteenth century.

At the outset of his public life, in 1841, Douglass quickly recognized the representative nature of a slave's individual experience: "During the first three or four months, my speeches were almost exclusively made up of narrations of my own personal experience as a slave. . . . It did not entirely satisfy me to *narrate* wrongs; I felt like *denouncing* them. I could not always curb my moral indignation for the perpetrators of slaveholding villainy, long enough for a circumstantial statement of the facts."[8] (The development of his own public identity and political strategy led Douglass to act independently of Garrison's American Anti-Slavery Society upon his return to the United States in 1847.)

The *Narrative* and Discourse

The impact of Douglass's *Narrative*, which remains undiminished today, derives from its emphatic correlations between narration and discourse. Narration in the book individuates his experience as a slave, while its discourse generalizes the experience. The *Narrative* thus mobilizes personal history to the political cause of abolition. For Douglass, the history of his individual enslavement implements denunciation of slavery and of its injustices to African-American humanity. His book's narrative endows actual events with a plot structure, and its discourse submits them as evidence in an indictment of slavery. As the *Narrative* recounts personal history, it progressively discloses the general human significance of that history.

The circumstances of a slave's birth bespeak the basic injustices of slavery. After stating the specific geographical place of his birth in the *Narrative*'s first sentence, Douglass continues: "I have no accurate knowledge of my age, never having seen any authentic record containing it. By far the larger part of the slaves know as little of their ages as horses know of theirs, and it is the wish of most masters within my knowledge to keep their slaves thus ignorant. I do not remember to have ever met a slave who could tell of his birthday" (*Narrative*, 21). These circumstances correlate the fact of a slave's existence with conditions that are inhuman, conditions that entail the deprivation of an individual *human* identity and of a humanizing knowledge of one's origins in time.

That deprivation applies as well to matters of family identity for the individual slave. Douglass records the separation, in infancy, from his mother Harriet Bailey. Masters often forced the breakup of the slave family as a matter of policy. Harriet Bailey was hired out as a field hand to a farmer whose lands were some twelve miles distant. Before her death, which occurred when he was about seven years old, Frederick was reunited with his mother only four or five times that he could remember. These few occasions were of short duration, and they occurred in the dead of night, for Harriet could not leave the fields during any daylight hours. She journeyed by foot and without the permission of her master, who had dictated the separation. Douglass points out the brutal irony that in the rare instances when such permission is granted it confers on the slaveowner "the proud name of being a kind master" (*Narrative*, 22).

Douglass states frankly in the *Narrative*, "My father was a white man. He was admitted to be such by all I ever heard speak of my parentage" (*Narrative*, 21). In the next autobiography, Douglass partially deflects the issue: "My father was a white man, or nearly white. It was sometimes whispered that my master was my father" (*My Bondage*, 52). His last autobiography reconceptualizes the matter: "Of my father I know nothing. Slavery had no recognition of fathers, as none of families."[9] Denied an acknowledged father, Frederick took the name of his mother's family as his last name. The modern standard biography, written by William S. McFeely, indicates that the family name Bailey is recorded in local slave documents for at least four generations prior to Frederick's birth.[10]

Though McFeely speculates that *Bailey* may have African roots, most often the institution of slavery assigned the white owner's name to identify specific slaves. That name was commonly recorded in deeds and other property documents as the slave's surname. Through sale to another master, that surname was often changed to that of the new owner. Instead of a sign of biological ties, the surname was a sign of the slave's property (or "chattel") status. In reaction against the historical injustice thus recorded in many African-American surnames, Malcolm X adopted the Black Muslim practice of symbolically crossing out his last name, as he memorably explains in his autobiography.

Like all slaves, Douglass had social legitimacy only as a white person's property. Denied the surname of his father, Douglass is born a bastard. The *Narrative* indicates through this individual circumstance that by definition the whole slave population is illegitimate at birth. It indicates further that his victimization as a slave was compounded by the fact of white paternity. Such racially mixed children provoked jealous hostility within the owner's marriage, and their presence created a situation where, as Douglass bitterly remarks, "it is often the dictate of humanity" for the master and father "to sell his own children to human flesh-mongers" (*Narrative*, 23). While he was not sold in this fashion, Frederick was removed at age eight from the plantation in rural Maryland to the Baltimore household of Hugh Auld. That same year, 1826, his first master and reputed white father Aaron Anthony died.

Frederick bore the surname Bailey until the time of his escape. En route to his eventual destination, New Bedford, he adopted the pseudonyms Stanley and Johnson. He married in New York in 1838 under the surname Johnson. His first sponsors in New Bedford—the African-American couple Mary and Nathan Johnson—encouraged Frederick to adopt a new last name since there were already so many individuals with that family name in the city. He accepted his sponsor's proposal of *Douglass*, adapted from the name of a heroic character in Sir Walter Scott's narrative poem *The Lady of the Lake*. This process of renaming is explained in the *Narrative*: "I gave Mr. Johnson the privilege of choosing me a name, but told him he must not take from me the name of 'Frederick.' I must hold on to that, to preserve a sense of identity. . . . From that time until now I have been called 'Frederick Douglass;' and as I am more widely known by that name than by either of the others, I shall continue to use it as my own" (114–15).

Douglass's explanation conveys the recognition that slavery has denied him a birthright and an intrinsic identity and that his public identity fills the existential void left by his origins as a slave. The *I* in discourse of the orator and autobiographer established the authority and authenticity of the individual to be identified historically as Frederick Douglass. Speaking and writing while he remained, by law, the property of a white Maryland family, Douglass acquired through discourse the individuality and subjectivity that enabled him to take possession of himself.

The encompassing existential destitution that starts with the slave's birth is reinforced by the physical deprivation and violence sanctioned by slavery. Douglass offers his personal memories as a legible record of brutality retained on the body and in the consciousness of the slave. The fact that most slaves are further deprived of any means to communicate such brutality through any literate form makes Douglass's account all the more powerfully representative. Hunger and cold were persistent enemies in childhood; the master's allotment of food and clothing were most deficient when the slave was too young for constant labor. The autobiographer conveys the indelible physical truth left on him by such brute conditions: "My feet have been so cracked with the frost, that the pen with which I am writing might be laid in the gashes" (*Narrative*, 43).

Douglass details one whipping he received from the overseer Edward Covey, and he records that for a period of six months during adolescence "scarce a week passed without his whipping me. I was seldom free from a sore back" (*Narrative*, 72). The slave's back was usually the target of such systematic violence in order to avoid permanently impairing the slave from work, as might happen if his or her limbs were injured. The whipping first reported in the *Narrative* is one received by his Aunt Hester and witnessed by Douglass in childhood. Probably he was no more than seven years old at the time. The event marks his birth into consciousness: "It was the blood-stained gate, the entrance to the hell of slavery, through which I was about to pass" (*Narrative*, 25). Her offense was to have left her quarters at night and to have been found in the company of a male slave. Master Anthony, in a rage of jealous possessiveness, stripped her naked to the waist and flogged her mercilessly. With the discursive aside "Why master was so careful of her may be safely left to conjecture," Douglass points to the sexual exploitation of the female slave (*Narrative*, 25). In the *Narrative*, Douglass conceives of his childhood as the product of such compounded victimization. The concept of himself as a slave child changes significantly in the later autobiographies.

Another whipping, recounted early in the *Narrative*, leads to murder. After a few strokes of the whip from the plantation overseer Austin Gore, the field slave Demby fled to a nearby creek to cool his wounds. After Demby did not respond to the order to return for further whipping, Gore raised his musket at the slave's head at close range. Without further warning, Gore's gunshot slaughtered Demby. After this intense narrative, Douglass discourses that such murders went unprosecuted since slaves had no legal status as human beings, not as victims nor as witnesses. In the face of disenfranchisement from any system of justice, Douglass employs the prose in his *Narrative* as a form of litigation: "Mr. Gore lived in St. Michael's, Talbot county, Maryland, when I left there; and if he is still alive, he very probably lives there now; and if so, he is now, as he was then, as highly esteemed and as much respected as though his guilty soul had not been stained with his brother's blood" (*Narrative*, 40–41). Douglass here simulates the language of a legal proceeding, specifically that of indictment and prosecution. He also asserts a standard of human rights ("his brother's blood") above all standards of statutory law.

Douglass's discourse in the *Narrative* is persuasive in its directness and clarity and in the craft of its argumentative statements. Austin Gore is presented, for example, as a man "eminent" in his possession of all the traits requisite for "a first-rate overseer": "Mr. Gore was proud, ambitious, and persevering. He was artful, cruel, and obdurate. He was just the man for such a place, and it was just the place for such a man" (*Narrative*, 38). Over the paragraph that follows, Douglass develops and intensifies the meaning of these summary statements without complicating or clouding that meaning. The paragraph continues, "He was just proud enough to demand the most debasing homage of the slave, and quite servile enough to crouch, himself, at the feet of the master. He was ambitious enough to be contented with nothing short of the highest rank of overseers, and persevering enough to reach the height of his ambition. He was cruel enough to inflict the severest punishment, artful enough to descend to the lowest trickery, and obdurate enough to be insensible to the voice of a reproving conscience" (*Narrative*, 39). Parallel structure and patterns of reiteration in these sentences sustain ironies that condemn the dehumanized standard of an overseer's success. The personality profile identifies in this white functionary of the slaveholding system a perversion of human values and ambitions and a psychological servility to the status and authority of the plantation owner.

Douglass's Growth and Liberation

In being transferred at age eight to Baltimore and the household of Hugh and Sophie Auld, Douglass was removed for a time from the plantation scenes of white barbarity. Douglass credits this turn of fate with his eventual liberation: "I have ever regarded it as the first plain manifestation of that kind providence which has ever since attended me, and marked my life with so many favors" (*Narrative*, 46–47). Though Douglass's eventual liberation entails remarkable acts of individual will, he honestly testifies to a higher agency because, in his view, he could not have overcome the inhumanity of slavery by individual human power alone. Malcolm X, another African-American of immense individual will, made similar testimony. In his *Autobiography*, Malcolm X comments on the extraordinary course his life has taken: "I believe that everything is written," he writes, in reference to the will of Allah.[11]

Sophie Auld had never had a slave in her management before, and she initially treated Frederick with a goodness that astonished him. She seemed disturbed by the abject habits of servility already ingrained in the child, and she encouraged his social and intellectual development. Her humane treatment ended abruptly when Hugh Auld discovered that his wife had begun to instruct Frederick in reading and spelling. He forbade all such instruction and warned her, "Learning would *spoil* the best nigger in the world" (*Narrative*, 49). Douglass reports that this condemnation struck him then as a "revelation": "The argument which he so warmly urged, against my learning to read, only served to inspire me with a desire and determination to learn" (*Narrative*, 49–50).

Douglass's aspiration to literacy is thus forged in revolt against slavery's restrictions. What his white master condemned, he knew to be indispensable. Southern states had adopted laws to maintain illiteracy in the slave populations. Humanely inclined white citizens like Sophie Auld were also obligated to conform to such laws. The dehumanizing effects of slavery thus extended into the white population. Douglass notes the corruption of Sophie Auld: "The fatal poison of irresponsible power was already in her hands, and soon commenced its infernal work. . . . Slavery proved as injurious to her as it did to me" (*Narrative*, 48, 52).

After his instruction was forbidden in the Auld household in Baltimore, Douglass undertook a difficult and dangerous project of self-education. Through a combination of ingenuity, indirection, and help from poor white children, oftentimes after bribing them with bread, Douglass achieved basic reading skill. At about age twelve he acquired a copy of *The Columbian Orator*, an American school reader that compiles examples of great speeches, from Cicero to George Washington. Intended to develop republican beliefs, *The Columbian Orator* contains many speeches on the cause of liberty, including that of American independence, the emancipation of Catholics, and freedom for American slaves.[12]

This inspiring oratory left Douglass, however, in a state of literacy without liberation that caused him to despair: "I would at times feel that learning to read had been a curse rather than a blessing. It had given me a view of my wretched condition, without the remedy" (*Narrative*, 55). In learning to write, Douglass resorted to further ploys, including a challenge to street boys to prove that they could write, after which he would imitate their script: "During this time, my copy-book was the board fence, brick wall, and pavement; my pen and ink was a lump of chalk" (*Narrative*, 58).

As it had for Benjamin Franklin, writing would prove instrumental for Douglass in the effort toward independence.[13] But independence for an African-American in the nineteenth century is a far different matter than independence was for a white American colonial male of Franklin's reputation. Douglass bears the scars of a slave's existence, while the adversities Franklin endured run no deeper than his own errata. Before Douglass could recreate himself in his autobiographies as a representative man, in life he first had to assert himself as a man in defiance of a culture that valued him only as movable property. Through writing and printing Franklin formed influential political ties that profited him. Through the same means Douglass managed to break his bondage, and through them he sought ultimately to deprive the slaveholding system of its means of profit.

The *Narrative* presents white authority figures like Gore and the Aulds as demonic agents. Disobedience and resistance to this authority charts the course of Douglass's eventual deliverance from slavery. At age fourteen Douglass was transferred back to the plantation. As a consequence of his contrary behavior, the Auld family leased Douglass to the local farmer Edward Covey, whose purpose was to break the young slave's spirit. For the first time in his life Douglass worked as a field hand, and, for his awkwardness at manual labor, he received frequent beatings over the first six months. This prolonged brutality led to the turning point in his life.

The discourse of the *Narrative* extensively employs the rhetorical device of antithesis to recount this turn of fate. Covey practiced elaborate secrecy and deceit in order to detect his slaves slackening at work: "Such was his cunning, that we used to call him, among ourselves, 'the snake.' . . . His comings were like a thief in the night" (*Narrative*, 73). While the first attribute is satanic, the second refers to New Testament imagery of the return of Christ to earth.[14] The paradoxical description of Covey sets the stage for Douglass's resurrection *within* the prevailing evil of slavery, which condemns master and slave alike.

Direct confrontation with Covey miraculously transformed Douglass: "You have seen how a man was made a slave; you shall see how a slave was made a man" (*Narrative*, 77). After another savage beating by Covey, Douglass fled and appealed to Master Thomas Auld for protection. Though Douglass was drenched in his own blood, the master denied that the slave was seriously injured or in danger of being killed. Douglass was sent back to Covey's farm. On the way, a fellow slave named Sandy Jenkins foraged in the woods for a root to be carried in Douglass's pocket as a protection against further beating. The day of his return, a Sunday, was one of unexpected peace. Had this unusual circumstance occurred on any day other than the Sabbath, Douglass admits, he might have placed trust in the root's powers.

But the next day, Covey took Douglass by surprise and attacked again. The *Narrative* records, "at this moment—from whence came the spirit I don't know—I resolved to fight" (*Narrative*, 81). His resistance was so unexpected and so determined that it soon caused Covey to back down. Victory in this skirmish was transfiguring: "It was a glorious resurrection, from the tomb of slavery, to the heaven of freedom. . . . I now resolved that, however long I might remain a slave in form, the day had passed forever when I could be a slave in fact" (*Narrative*, 83). Over the remaining six months of the lease to Covey that year, Douglass received no further beatings.

The *Narrative* explains that Christian zeal made Covey maniacal in his position as master. It was Covey's conviction that religious sanction gave him the absolute right to brutalize slaves under his control. Douglass's aversion as an abolitionist to such a profanation of Christian principles led him to conclude the *Narrative* not with an account of events but with a summary statement on this matter. In the book's appendix, Douglass declares: "I therefore hate the corrupt, slaveholding, women-whipping, cradle-plundering, partial and hypocritical Christianity of this land" (*Narrative*, 120). The indictment charges Christians of the North along with those of the South with betraying the "Christianity of Christ" (*Narrative*, 120). Abolitionist leaders, many of them Northern ministers, exhorted Americans to adhere to the humanitarianism in Christ's teachings as a law higher than that of government.

No security against the brutality of slavery was afforded Douglass by the authority of Master Auld or by the superstitions of Sandy Jenkins. Instead, literacy later empowered Douglass to write "protections" for himself and a small group of slaves in his first escape attempt, which Douglass dates to 1835 (*Narrative*, 94). The "protections" were passes, reputedly from a local master, forged to explain the distant travel of these unescorted slaves. Learning of the escape plan through an informant, the owner and local constables placed Douglass and the others under arrest. In trying to conceal their collaboration, one of the group ingested his forged pass. Before they could be questioned by authorities, the captured slaves exchanged the whispered caution "*Own nothing!*" (*Narrative*, 97). The phrase is tellingly metaphoric of their dispossession.

By tradition, the *Narrative* relates, slavery granted a counterfeit liberty during the week between Christmas and New Year's

Day, when slaves were freed from labors other than tending live-stock. The sober and industrious among the slaves would employ the free time in efforts to make their quarters livable. Masters encouraged slaves to indulge instead in diversions, mer-riment, and dissipation—from sports to drinking whiskey. Douglass maintains that the master considered it a personal insult for slaves not to indulge themselves: "He was regarded as one who rejected the favor of his master. It was deemed a dis-grace not to get drunk at Christmas" (*Narrative*, 84).

Douglass reasons that the false liberties of the holiday season aid the system of slavery in dissipating the slave's desire for free-dom and the spirit of insurrection. In a public address, "What to the Slave is the Fourth of July?" delivered in 1852, Douglass makes a similar assessment of the nation's Independence Day celebrations. Though himself legally a freedman by this time, Douglass states that while American slavery exists "I am not included within the pale of this glorious anniversary! Your high independence only reveals the immeasurable distance between us. . . . This Fourth of July is *yours*, not *mine*."[15] His address con-cludes with a summary statement of America's "national incon-sistencies. The existence of slavery in this country brands your republicanism as a sham, your humanity as a base pretence, and your Christianity as a lie" (*Papers*, 383).

The pursuit of liberty is conceived by Douglass as a collective effort and never simply as an individual matter. The only possible means for slaves to assemble publicly for a common purpose was in religious meetings. But even this purpose was held in suspi-cion by slaveholders. Douglass reports that during his bondage on the Auld plantation in 1832, a well-meaning young white man started a Sabbath school for the purpose of instructing slaves to read the New Testament. After three meetings, however, leaders in the local Methodist church disbanded the group through force and threatened worse violence should it reconvene.

Two years later Auld hired Douglass out to a farm owned by William Freeland, a name whose irony resonates for the autobi-ographer: "By this time, I began to want to live *upon free land*" (*Narrative*, 91). Douglass started a Sabbath school and "accord-ingly devoted my Sundays to teaching these my loved fellow-slaves how to read" (*Narrative*, 89). Before long the school drew upward of 40 adults. It was the role of instructor, not the Bible they studied, that provided Douglass with spiritual fulfillment: "It was the delight of my soul to be doing something that looked like bettering the condition of my race" (*Narrative*, 90).

At this time, Douglass and a group of five other slaves resolved upon an escape attempt, the first one Douglass made, in 1835. Sandy Jenkins, one member of the group, soon abandoned the idea. Each remaining member was placed under arrest on the day of their intended flight. The *Narrative* states that one person had alerted a master of the escape plan. Without naming that person, Douglass concludes, "we came to a unanimous decision among ourselves as to who their informant was" (*Narrative*, 97). The account given in *My Bondage and My Freedom* and repeated in *Life and Times*, however, continues: "Several circumstances seemed to point Sandy out, as our betrayer. . . . And yet, we could not suspect him. We all loved him too well to think it *possible* that he could have betrayed us. So we rolled the guilt on other shoulders" (*My Bondage*, 297). This statement reveals an emotional need for solidarity that overrides his own rational conclusion.

The *Narrative* eloquently pleads the shared cause of abolition. In appending his name to the last page of the *Narrative*, Douglass makes a public pledge: "Sincerely and earnestly hoping that this little book may do something toward throwing light on the American slave system, and hastening the glad day of deliverance to the millions of my brethren in bonds" (*Narrative*, 126). Douglass maintains such solidarity in the *Narrative* through discourse, while through historical narration he chronicles only one individual's successful resistance and escape. For Frederick Douglass, personal history ends where public life as an orator begins, and the *Narrative* ultimately derives from that public life. The *Narrative* reincorporates personal history in the cause of collective liberation for the African-American slave.

Harriet Jacobs

Incidents in the Life of a Slave Girl (1861) by Harriet Jacobs also relates literacy with liberty in profound ways. Her first owner was a gentle and generous woman who extended maternal concern toward the slave girl. But her white mistress died when

Harriet Jacobs was less than twelve years old. Harriet had hoped that the mistress's last act of kindness would mean emancipation for herself, but the woman's will bequeathed her as a slave to a niece in the family, a child five years old at the time. The narrative to *Incidents in the Life of a Slave Girl* opens with an account of these events in order to record her life's first lesson in slavery's inhumanity.

Assessing this period of life now some thirty years later, and from the perspective of her physical freedom, Jacobs writes: "I would give much to blot out from my memory that one great wrong. As a child, I loved my mistress; and, looking back on the happy days I spent with her, I try to think with less bitterness of this act of injustice. While I was with her, she taught me to read and spell; and for this privilege, which so rarely falls to the lot of a slave, I bless her memory."[16] The irony in this assessment is that now her literacy enables Jacobs to record the mistress's injustice. In this discursive formulation, literacy itself is the true blessing.

Harriet Jacobs was relocated as a slave to the household of Dr. and Mrs. Flint, parents to the niece named in the will. Though her new owners forbade formal instruction for slaves, Harriet advanced in social literacy: "Those years had brought much of the knowledge that comes from experience, though they had afforded little opportunity for any other kinds of knowledge" (*Incidents*, 28). This social knowledge included the sexual exploitation of female slaves by their masters, which Dr. Flint attempted to initiate by the time Harriet turned fifteen. Jacobs met Flint's verbal harassment with pretended ignorance. When he put his sexual intimidation in writing, she feigned illiteracy.

While a teenager, Harriet managed, in private, to teach herself to write. During this time, she was asked by a pious old African-American man to instruct him so that he could finally read the Bible on his own. Before she agreed to do so, Harriet reminded the man of the dangers to both of them should whites discover such instruction. She made this warning not to dissuade him but to emphasize their need for vigilance. Their success in his acquisition of literacy brought to the old man spiritual joy and to Harriet a sense of reverence in humanity.

At age twenty-one, Harriet Jacobs fled from the Flint family and concealed herself in the vicinity. Soon Harriet installed herself in a cramped hiding place inside her grandmother's house. The autobiographer terms this garret space her "loophole of retreat" (*Incidents*, 173). From this retreat she maintained clandestine contact with her family. Harriet also arranged for a letter she wrote to be sent to Dr. Flint from New York in order to disguise her actual presence within his immediate vicinity in the South. To authenticate her claim, she took information from a recent Northern newspaper. The autobiography explains, with satisfaction: "It was a piece of the New York *Herald*; and, for once, the paper that systematically abuses the colored people was made to render them a service" (*Incidents*, 194).

Harriet's "loophole" was a kind of living tomb from which she emerged seven years later to escape North. Once she reached New York, however, Harriet recognized the necessity of learning to read the cultural meaning of sights and events in the urban North, including the reality of segregation in the "free" states. In the 1850s the "freedom" of Harriet Jacobs (that is, her *person*, as property) was purchased by a Northern benefactor, without her prior knowledge or approval. At the close of her narrative, Jacobs reflects on her "free papers": "The bill of sale is on record, and future generations will learn from it that women were articles of traffic in New York, late in the nineteenth century of the Christian religion. It may hereafter prove a useful document to antiquaries, who are seeking to measure the progress of civilization in the United States. I well know the value of that bit of paper; but much as I love freedom, I do not like to look upon it" (*Incidents*, 300–301). In this circumstance, her literacy and her liberty remain a paradoxical legacy.

Richard Wright

At the time in childhood when Richard Wright began to learn words and numbers he also began to learn the meaning of the color line in segregated America of the 1910s, as he recounts in *Black Boy* (1945). Though anxiety left him unable to speak when called upon in the classroom, Richard quickly learned the obscenities spoken by older black boys on the playground. The future novelist "published" his first words by writing these obscenities in soap on all the neighborhood windows. The first story to influence his imagination was "Bluebeard and His Seven Wives," recited to him by a boarder in his grandmother's house. The tale answered a desire in him for intrigue, secrecy, and violence: the "whispered story of deception and murder had been the first experience in my life that had elicited from me a total emotional response."[17] It awakened in the black boy a consciousness already dulled by the effects of racism in the American South.

One day while his grandmother was giving him a bath, Richard uttered an obscene comment. The words provoked shock, outrage, and a severe beating from his family, though Richard was ignorant of their real meaning. The experience reinforced his attraction to the power of forbidden language and thoughts. His natural childhood curiosity in matters of his own identity, of race, and of segregation was met with equal hostility by his mother. Family punishment and the refrain "Quit asking questions," heard throughout boyhood, forged in Richard the resolve "that in the future I would learn the meaning of why they had beat and denounced me" (*Black Boy*, 157, 53).

Black Boy presents the childhood and adolescent years of Wright's socialization within the system of segregation and lynch law as a life of negative vitality. Wright the autobiographer endows the black boy with existential heroism: "At the age of twelve, before I had had one full year of formal schooling I had . . . a conviction that the meaning of living came only when one was struggling to wring a meaning out of meaningless suffering" (*Black Boy*, 112). By age nineteen, Wright was waging that struggle through tireless reading. He had to engage in forgery and subterfuge to gain access to the public library, barred to him by the color line.

Reading answered the old hunger to know and stimulated a new one: "I now knew what being a Negro meant. I could endure the hunger. I had learned to live with hate. But to feel that there were feelings denied me, that the very breath of life itself was beyond my reach, that more than anything else hurt, wounded me. I had a new hunger" (*Black Boy*, 274). This phase concludes with Wright's departure from the South for Chicago in 1927, the point in life history where *Black Boy* also reaches its conclusion. The new hunger could be answered only through becoming a writer, a process presented in the continuation of Wright's autobiography, *American Hunger* (1945).[18]

The urban North required of Wright another kind of social literacy: "I was persisting in reading my present environment in the light of my old one" (*Hunger*, 5). His mature understanding of American society evolved through various jobs he took—most profoundly as a salesman of insurance and burial policies to poor black families and as a social worker with the Boys Club in Chicago's South Side—and through the political education provided by the American Communist Party. During the association with the Party, his hunger to write evolved into efforts at imaginative literature. The truths that he began to reach through fiction were at odds with Communist doctrine, and his gradual estrangement from the Party started.

American Hunger ends when Wright's destiny as a writer is cast: "I would hurl words into this darkness and wait for an echo, and if an echo sounded, no matter how faintly, I would send other words to tell, to march, to fight, to create a sense of the hunger for life that gnaws in us all, to keep alive in our hearts a sense of the inexpressibly human" (*Hunger*, 135). Through this aspiration toward universality, Richard Wright went forward to become a novelist with a masterful capacity to articulate African-American experience across all color lines.

Malcolm X

As recounted in *The Autobiography of Malcolm X*, Malcolm X attained social literacy in the ways of segregated America well before he acquired, in prison, full literacy in language. In the early 1940s, working on passenger trains as a sandwich man, he soon recognized that along with the other porters and waiters he occupied "that world of Negroes who are both servants and psychologists, aware that white people are so obsessed with their own importance that they will pay liberally, even dearly, for the impression of being catered to and entertained" (*Malcolm*, 75).

On one train trip he was confronted by a drunken white soldier who blocked the aisle and announced "I'm going to fight you, nigger" (*Malcolm*, 77). Malcolm agreed to fight, but he suggested that the soldier might want to remove his bulky Army overcoat first. Malcolm cheerfully encouraged him to remove further articles of his uniform until the drunken GI was stripped to the waist. In this condition the soldier was a laughingstock to the other passengers, and his Army buddies pulled him away. The experience provided an invaluable lesson: "I never would forget that—that I couldn't have whipped that white man as badly with a club as I had with my mind" (*Malcolm*, 77).

Malcolm X did not undertake a systematic development of his mind until his long prison term, from 1946 to 1952. After admiring the eloquence of a respected African-American convict, Malcolm decided that he needed to acquire a vocabulary beyond the street language in which he then spoke. Faced with the new, vast world of language in a dictionary, he began to copy the book, page by page and verbatim. Once a page was copied, he studied its contents closely. He proceeded through the entire dictionary in this fashion. The dictionary thus provided this novice reader an encyclopedia of knowledge. As his reading and reflection branched out to other books, Malcolm X experienced the first sensation of being "truly free" in his life (*Malcolm*, 173). The liberation of his consciousness made more acute his awareness of the disenfranchisement of African-Americans: "My homemade education gave me, with every additional book that I read, a little bit more sensitivity to the deafness, dumbness, and blindness that was afflicting the black race in America" (*Malcolm*, 179). From this point until its conclusion, the narrative to *The Autobiography of Malcolm X* is a history of Malcolm X's "salvation" through his public life as an orator, first as a debater among fellow convicts, then as a minister for the Black Muslims, and finally as leader of his newly formed Organization of Afro-American Unity. Like the Douglass *Narrative*, *The Autobiography of Malcolm X* is both the life story of one of America's great orators and a brilliant instance of the social and cultural powers of African-American oratory.

With these examples, it is evident that the matter of literacy in African-American autobiography does not remain at the pragmatic and superficial level that E. D. Hirsch proposes as the acceptable standard of cultural literacy in America. Our nation's history of slavery and its legacies of segregation and the color line have led many African-American autobiographers, in their acquisition of literacy, to confront the contradictions between American social reality and the country's founding political ideals. For the slave, language acquisition was inevitably accompanied by awareness of the prohibitions against such mental development. That awareness in turn contributed to the slave's developing social literacy. For the nearly 100 years from emancipation to the civil rights movement initiated in the 1950s, African-Americans continued to read the double messages of a segregated society in learning to read the word.

4

The Autobiographies of Gertrude Stein

Questions of Self

O n her deathbed Gertrude Stein turned to Alice Toklas, her companion of forty years, and asked in a whisper: "What is the answer?" Unable to guess what Stein, under sedation for her severe pain, might mean by the query, Toklas remained silent. Stein continued: "In that case, what is the question?"[1] Her famous dying words, delivered in 1946, have long helped identify the personality and imagination of Gertrude Stein, one of the first and most important modernist experimenters in literature, for a public that largely has not read her experimental work. Her two autobiographies—*The Autobiography of Alice B. Toklas* (1933) and *Everybody's Autobiography* (1937)—are offered to that general public as explorations into questions of personal identity and into conventions of the genre.

Gertrude Stein's *The Autobiography of Alice B. Toklas* is a paradoxical example of autobiography. In its first edition, the autobiography presented only the title on the cover and the title page.

The book's concluding paragraph, however, narrates a situation that many readers will have come to suspect early on: "About six weeks ago Gertrude Stein said, it does not look to me as if you were ever going to write that autobiography. You know what I am going to do. I am going to write it for you. . . . And she has and this is it."[2] The book thus doubles as an autobiography of Toklas, written by Stein on behalf of Toklas, and a biography of Stein, written by Stein in the person of Toklas. This second feature makes the book a distinctive instance of autobiography in the third person.[3] Each party to *The Autobiography of Alice B. Toklas* subsequently wrote an autobiography in her proper person, Stein with *Everybody's Autobiography* and Toklas with *What Is Remembered* (1963).[4]

In *Toklas*, the guise of an autobiography by Alice B. Toklas shifts within three pages to a biography of Stein, which, since the book is authored by Stein, requalifies the book as an autobiography, though the point of view remains ostensibly that of Toklas throughout. The shift is marked by "Toklas's" statement: "I may say that only three times in my life have I met a genius . . . and I may say in each case it was before there was any general recognition of the quality of genius in them. The three geniuses of whom I wish to speak are Gertrude Stein, Pablo Picasso and Alfred Whitehead" (*Stein*, 5). A similar pantheon of three is proposed later, with André Gide substituted for Whitehead, and Stein's reaction is reported as: "that is quite right but why include Gide" (*Stein*, 231).

In their Paris apartment and atelier, Toklas entertained the wives of famous visitors while Stein was occupied in the company of fellow artists and celebrities. Toklas is made to say: "Before I decided to write this book my twenty-five years with Gertrude Stein, I had often said that I would write The wives of geniuses I have sat with" (*Stein*, 13). Through such ironies, *The Autobiography of Alice B. Toklas* makes indirect acknowledgment of the devoted lesbian marriage enjoyed by Toklas and Stein. The moral and censorship standards of the era prohibited any published discussion of their relationship more frank than this. Gertrude Stein defies the proscriptions and stereotypes based on gender during the era, but in the autobiographies she does not identify herself in solidarity with the cause of women. Though unengaged by ideology or political action, Stein nevertheless asserts a feminism through her inalienable consciousness of self.

With *The Autobiography of Alice B. Toklas*, Stein performs variations on her modernist prose experiments, now made more comfortably accessible for the reader through a tone of domestic familiarity in the assumed voice of Toklas. A full statement of Stein's modernist methods is provided in the essay "Composition as Explanation," first delivered in 1926 as a lecture at Cambridge and Oxford Universities, England. Stein wrote this statement one afternoon in 1925 in a garage as her Ford car was being dismantled and reassembled by a mechanic. By the time the automobile was repaired she had finished writing it. The Ford motor car, as a product of assembly-line techniques and the standardization of interchangeable parts, is an apt counterpart to the qualities of modern composition she endorses. In a self-portrait, Stein describes herself as particularly fond of working in the automobile while it remained parked in busy Paris streets.

For Stein *composition* is a quality inclusive of social experience and culture: "Each period of living differs from any other period . . . in the way life is conducted and that authentically speaking is composition" (*Stein*, 517). For the modern period, the composition of experience manifests at least three distinctive properties: "a continuous present and using everything and beginning again" (*Stein*, 518). The compositional effect is fully apparent in her "Three Portraits of Painters" (1912). A representative sentence from the prose portrait of Picasso reads: "One whom some were certainly following and some were certainly following him, one whom some were certainly following was one certainly working" (*Stein*, 334). The sentence structure is serial in its patterns of repetition and reiteration.

Time and Language

These modernist properties conflict with traits of chronology and individuality conventional to autobiography in the historical mode. The chapter "My Arrival in Paris" in *The Autobiography of Alice B. Toklas*, for example, begins with Toklas's stated intention to chronicle the events of 1907 in her life. From the outset, however, its narrative drifts to subjects such as the French maidservant Hélène, Hélène's marriage, the maid's opinions on painters like Matisse and Braque, and her experiences since the conclusion of World War I. Though Toklas has promised to discuss her reactions to the paintings hanging in the Stein atelier when she first saw them in 1907, these digressions require her to renew the promise. In the course of two paragraphs, for instance, she curtails one digression only to be led into new ones: "But to come back to 1907. . . . But to return to the pictures. . . . But this time I am really going to tell about the pictures" (*Stein*, 8–9). Her dislocations in the contexts of time and place become comic and charming.

The Autobiography of Alice B. Toklas offers temporal references and dates in every chapter title (such as "Gertrude Stein Before She Came to Paris" and "1907–1914"), and it maintains a broad chronological progression from beginning to end. In the structure of its prose, however, the autobiography does not establish a cumulative sequence of events over time in order to provide a causal explanation of life experience. In its drift, *Toklas* defies the conventions of historical narrative.

Time is treated in the autobiography as a relative, mobile medium. The time in which *Toklas* was composed becomes part of its reconstitution of time past. In recounting events of 1907, Toklas remarks, "Many years after, that is just a few years ago" (*Stein*, 19). While telling of her second meeting with Pablo Picasso and his wife Fernande, Toklas anticipates the end of their marriage in the near future. But she stops herself before taking this narrative detour: "I will tell the whole story as I afterward learnt it but now I must find Fernande and propose to her to take french lessons from her" (*Stein*, 18). The *now* in this sentence is double-voiced: it refers both to the imperative of relating the next event in composing the narrative and to the chronology of events *within* the narrative.

In "Composition as Explanation," this duality is termed "the time of the composition and the time in the composition" (*Stein*, 516). It conveys a modernity introduced by American experience. Stein has Toklas state, from her perspective in 1933: "America created the twentieth century, and since all the other countries are now either living or commencing to be living a twentieth century life, America having begun the creation of the twentieth century in the sixties of the nineteenth is now the oldest country in the world" (*Stein*, 73).

Though a resident of France from 1903, at age twenty-nine, until the end of her life in 1946, Stein always considered herself a representative modern American. Stein explains the advantages of being an American writer who is an expatriate: "One of the things that I have liked all these years is to be surrounded by people who know no english. It has left me more intensely alone with my eyes and my english. I do not know if it would have been possible to have english be so all in all to me otherwise" (*Stein*, 66). The autobiography reports that when surrounded by the sounds of spoken English, as during a visit to London for a few weeks in 1913, Stein was deeply vexed.

From Stein's perspective as a writer, the American language is inherently modern, and most obviously so in its expression through mass media such as advertising. In her opinion, American English exhibits a modern disconnection from the material, ordinary realities of life. Its words are detached from the solidity of the things and conditions to which they refer. In the lecture *Narration* (1935), Stein states the difference between traditional English and the American language as follows: "In the case of the English the words have the feeling of containing that in which they are staying and with the American they have the feeling that they are and indicate and feel moving existing inside in them."[5] Her statement is itself a demonstration in the American properties of language. With a word choice and syntax suggestive of colloquial speech, the sentence presents an appearance of a naïve American vernacular.[6] The simplicity of these words and the active verbal forms, as much as their import, structures the sentence.

Her statement stresses the processes and movement of language. The sentence is a working example of the continuous actual present, as in the accent on present participial forms and their conjunction in the phrase "feel moving existing." Stein terms the qualities embodied in American language "the American thing": "It is something strictly American to conceive a space that is filled with moving, a space of time that is filled always filled with moving" (*Stein*, 258). For Stein, as a consequence of her self-consciousness as a modern and American writer, her own autobiography cannot conform to the genre's conventions of retrospection and narration.

A former student of William James, the American philosopher and psychologist, Stein considers past experience to be part of the nontemporal continuum of consciousness. The past is not preserved in one's mind along linear tracks from its origins to the present. Instead, mind is a faculty of epic actuality. The mind contains the past as an immediate movement of experience rather than as data distant in time. The wholeness of the mind's stream of consciousness, in whose currents the past moves, is difficult to convey in conventional English because its syntax is normatively temporal and linear in structure.

One of Stein's major experiments with epic actuality is her prose narrative *The Making of Americans*, written in the period 1906–1908, first published in 1925. In 1935 Stein explained the challenge in writing such a book: "I had acquired all this knowledge gradually but when I had it I had it completely at one time. . . . [It] was a struggle to do this thing, to make a whole present of something it had taken a great deal of time to find out, but it was a whole there then within me and as such it had to be said" (*Stein*, 249). Her autobiographies pursue this aim through the kind of narrative mobility in time and context that has been cited. They convey her personal history with as much emphasis on the wholeness of present experience as on a resynthesis of the past.

Stein's celebrated phrase "a rose is a rose is a rose is a rose" embodies another quality of American language (*Stein*, 129). The *Toklas* autobiography explains that Toklas discovered the expression in one of Stein's manuscripts and then urged that it be used as an inscription on Stein's table linens and personal stationery. The phrase is powerfully modern in its detachment of *rose* from all prior cultural and literary contexts. These contexts date at least from the medieval symbolism of love in *Romance of the Rose* up through Romantic poets like Robert Burns ("O My Luve's like a red, red rose"). Ralph Waldo Emerson evokes an idealist, transcendental context when he states in the essay "Self-Reliance" (1841): "These roses under my window make no reference to former roses or to better ones; they are for what they are; they exist with God today."[7]

The Stein motto "a rose is a rose is a rose is a rose" can be considered a modern answer to the speculation on language and meaning formulated by Shakespeare: "What's in a name? that which we call a rose/By any other name would smell as sweet" (*Romeo and Juliet* 2.2.43–44). In the Stein motto, *rose* is detached from any symbol or living thing outside the part of speech itself. She later explained that through the phrase "I caressed completely caressed and addressed a noun."[8] This gratification in plain-spoken language reflects her basic principle that "the normal is so much more simply complicated and interesting" than the unusual or abnormal (*Stein*, 78). In their subject matter, many of the modern painters and sculptors Stein admired were making a similar discovery.

Nonrepresentation and Narration

For Gertrude Stein, writing thus is not a mode of direct representation of—nor one of direct reference to—experience and objective reality outside writing itself. Her nonrepresentational principles are clarified in the *Toklas* autobiography through the account of Picasso's portrait of Stein, completed in 1906. The painting is credited with leading a revolution in modern art: "In the long struggle with the portrait of Gertrude Stein, Picasso passed from the Harlequin, the charming early italian period to the intensive struggle which was to end in cubism" (*Stein*, 50).

Stein first sat for the portrait in the winter of 1905. The sketch Picasso completed for her first sitting was considered very beautiful by everyone who saw it, but as his image of Stein on the canvas changed over the months no one could recall what that first impression looked like. During the winter and spring months Stein posed for the one painting in some eighty to ninety sittings. Before departing for a summer vacation in Spain, Picasso became dissatisfied with the composition and completely painted out her head. In leaving the portrait's most important feature blank, Picasso complained "I can't see you any longer when I look" (*Stein*, 49). Immediately upon his return from Spain in autumn, Picasso painted the head of Gertrude Stein and finished the portrait without any further sittings by her. The distinctively monumental and masklike features of the painting convey a concept more than a likeness of Stein. Picasso has "caressed" Stein as if she were a noun—or the painterly equivalent, in form and color.

The autobiography identifies these same months as a period of great innovation in literature achieved by Gertrude Stein through her fictional narratives in *Three Lives* (first published in 1909). Echoing a tribute from a French critic, *Toklas* claims that in this novel "by exactitude, austerity, absence of variety in light and shade, by refusal of the use of the subconscious Gertrude Stein achieves a symmetry" (*Stein*, 47). These qualities also shape Stein's self-portraiture in *The Autobiography of Alice B. Toklas*. An external and objective method is attained through the use of Toklas for perspective on the self. The Toklas *persona*, or dramatic mask, narrates life at a surface level of the prose medium. The uniform patterns in language maintain an impression of depthlessness in the subject matter. By means of simplification and an avoidance of associational emotion, the narration of experience becomes a matter of dispassionate description.

The medium of language and the writer's conceptions through that medium are more important than experience itself for Stein—even in autobiography, a genre traditionally based in individual experience. Thus external reality cannot serve her as a model to be represented through writing. Rather, the writer projects a textual reality based on her particular, selective perspective: "Gertrude Stein . . . sticks strictly to general principles, the way of seeing what the writer chooses to see, and the relation between that vision and the way it gets down" (*Stein*, 202). These principles restate Picasso's resolution to the problem of his Stein painting, finished in her absence. Such vision is directed as much to the medium itself and to the artist's consciousness of self as it is to any separable subject matter.

The concerns for the actuality of consciousness and of the writing process in Stein's autobiographies largely exclude the dimensions of history, vital to Franklin's *Autobiography*, and the issues of social identity, inescapable in African-American autobiography. The suffering and devastation caused throughout Europe by World War I generally remain unperceived in *The Autobiography of Alice B. Toklas*. Among the civilians with whom Stein and Toklas continued to socialize, attitudes of nonchalance and naïveté persisted. They considered war a kind of tourist attraction with its own souvenirs, such as steel arrows and shell fragments. In the summer and fall of 1914 Toklas and Stein remained in London and the English countryside, while in the Marne valley French forces defended against a German attack headed toward Paris. Though *Toklas* makes mention of the massive battle of the Marne several times, its account of events is limited to three inconsequential reports from civilian friends.

The autobiography thus avoids any pretense of knowledge about events Stein has not participated in or witnessed. The book does convey an oblique and detached sense of self left by the war. The collective legacy for civilian and soldier alike was the destruction of ideals like patriotism and religion as passions for the young generation. It was this condition that prompted the statement "You are all a lost generation," attributed to Gertrude Stein and which Ernest Hemingway used as an inscription to his novel of postwar disillusionment *The Sun Also Rises* (1926). In *Everybody's Autobiography*, Stein explains that she heard the statement made first by a Frenchman.

In the south of France, far from actual combat, Toklas and Stein visited military hospitals and provided relief supplies to refugees during the last two years of war. Yet this contact with its victims leaves no graphic impression in the autobiography. In an automobile trip taken after the 1918 armistice, Toklas and Stein encountered firsthand the battlefields and trench lines to the east of Paris that had been recently abandoned. *Toklas* reports their reaction: "It was not terrifying it was strange. We were used to ruined houses and even ruined towns but this was different. It was a landscape. And it belonged to no country" (*Stein*, 176). The description captures the immediacy of a visual and conceptual impression, but not the experiential reality of the war just concluded.

In viewing munitions, gun emplacements, and military vehicles, Stein sees patterns of abstract composition, not the implements of war. Camouflage, for instance, is remarkable because among the several nations at war "the color schemes were different, the designs were different, the way of placing them was different, it made plain the whole theory of art and its inevitability" (*Stein*, 177). When Picasso first saw camouflaged cannons he exclaimed "we have created that," meaning that he and other modern painters had already produced such images. Stein agrees: "And he was right, he had. From Cezanne through him they had come to that" (*Stein*, 85). World War I made globally apparent the vision present earlier only in the modern arts: "War came . . . and so created the completed recognition of the contemporary composition" (*Stein*, 521). Stein defines modern composition by the values of exactitude, description, and reflexive forms and by an avoidance of emotional coloring. Such values are made obvious in the work of Picasso, Braque, Picabia, and other modernist painters and in the surface of Hemingway's prose.

The same values at times produce in Stein's social outlook an incapacity for understanding and a lack of compassion. On the issue of American race relations, the *Toklas* autobiography declares: "Gertrude Stein concluded that negroes were not suffering from persecution, they were suffering from nothingness" (*Stein*, 224). This statement comes in the autobiography as a response to a remark by the great African-American actor Paul Robeson, who had expressed gratitude that he had not been born in the South. As such, her statement willfully overlooks the realities of segregation and lynch law in American society to which Robeson referred. In more general terms, by "nothingness" Stein means an isolation from modern actuality or cultural change: "The african is not primitive, he has a very ancient but a very narrow culture and there it remains. Consequently nothing does or can happen" (*Stein*, 224). Stein's political outlook is not in any sense experimental or progressive.

Self and Consciousness

The questions of self and identity inescapably raised by the composition of modern experience propel the narrative to Stein's *Everybody's Autobiography*. The problem is put plainly there, in words that echo a nursery rhyme: "I became worried about identity and remembered the Mother Goose, I am I because my little dog knows me and I was not sure but that that only proved the dog was he and not that I was I."[9] Through the vernacular, Stein treats as "simply complicated" an issue that has perplexed philosophers. Issues of self have been redefined, since the modern era is no longer an age of individualism or subjectivity. Instead, it is an era of atomized, detached, and, at the same time, global identity.

Stein provides such reasons in explaining the title to her second autobiography: "There is really no relation between any one and so if this Everybody's Autobiography is to be the Autobiography of every one it is not to be of any connection between any one and any one because now there is none" (*Everybody's Autobiography*, 99). The title's *everybody* thus refers to an individual situation universally shared rather than to any collective identity. The book refers here to a modern condition of interchangeability and a society that lacks human cohesion. Stein presents this condition of anomie, which is terrifying for a modern writer like Franz Kafka, without a trace of anxiety or psychological disorientation. In fact, her prose delights in the modern condition, for it opens composition in the direction of "using everything."

While the genre traditionally privileges memory over the autobiographer's other faculties, Stein considers memory to be the least representative dimension of her consciousness and vision. Memory is incompatible with the compositional principles of "a continuous present . . . and beginning again." *Everybody's Autobiography* provides some recollections of Stein's family life in America and of the relationship with her brothers and sister, but these are limited to material that retains for her a sense of actuality and a relatively neutral objectivity.

In a moment of indirect emotional confession, Stein reveals a reason for her limited use of memory: "As I say fathers are depressing any father who is a father or any one who is a father and there are far too many fathers now existing. The periods of the world's history that have always been most dismal ones are the ones where fathers were looming and filling up everything. I had a father" (*Everybody's Autobiography*, 133). In the context of contemporary history, she names the fascists Hitler and Mussolini and the dictators Stalin and Franco as oppressive patriarchs. In the context of family history, she limits the narrative and description to her father's declining business fortunes and to a mention of his habitual anger, directed mainly toward her brother Mike. The autobiography leaves the matter of her father with a mention of his death, which occurred when she was seventeen, and its consequences: "Then our life without a father began a

(*Everybody's Autobiography*, 50). The suggestion by a friend that Stein might profit by composing cigarette advertisements led her to experiment with the form, but she had no resolve to market the prose that resulted.

On board the ocean liner taking her to the United States in 1934, Stein reflected: "I used to say that I would not go to America until I was a real lion a real celebrity at that time of course I did not really think I was going to be one. But now we were coming and I was going to be one. In America everybody is but some are more than others. I was more than others" (*Everybody's Autobiography*, 168). But Stein remained aware of the insecurity of celebrity: "America, which was supposed to be a land of success, was a land of failure" (*Everybody's Autobiography*, 86). Her concern was to preserve her authentic self, her textual self as a writer, distinct from the self made by publicity.

During her lecture tour of America in 1934–1935, Stein attracted enthusiastic audiences. Her preparation of these lectures had helped break a period of difficulty in her writing life, which the second autobiography traces to the public's acclaim for *The Autobiography of Alice B. Toklas*. Celebrity brought Stein into a life now defined outside herself and her writing. The book unexpectedly gained Stein a windfall income in royalties, which she quickly spent on a new Ford automobile and luxuries. But sudden success also entailed unaccustomed costs to her habitual detachment and to her sense of self. The months following publication of *Toklas* became a period of prolonged inactivity for Stein as a writer. Faced by such an impairment for the first time in her writing life, Stein started to question her identity: "It was then I began to think about am I I because my little dog knows me" (*Everybody's Autobiography*, 85). These consequences of success for a writer reverse the mythic pattern of Benjamin Franklin's public life, autobiography, and American identity.

On a visit to Hollywood during 1935, Stein explained the secret of her recent fame to a gathering of movie people that included Charlie Chaplin. Her explanation involves a fundamental difference between the mass media and literary art: "They wanted the publicity and the big audience, and really to have the biggest publicity you have to have a small one, yes all right the biggest publicity comes from the realest poetry and the realest poetry has a small audience not a big one, but it is really exciting and therefore it has the biggest publicity" (*Everybody's Autobiography*, 284). The autobiography reports that her statement baffled the movie people, who could think only in terms of box office revenues.

Stein writes *Everybody's Autobiography* with an awareness that, by her own literary standards, she is trading on personality. After *Toklas*, autobiography involves concessions to publicity: "Now how can you dream about a personality when it is always being created for you by a publicity, how can you believe what you make up when publicity makes them up to be so much realer than you can dream. And so autobiography is written which is in a way a way to say that publicity is right, they are as the public sees them" (*Everybody's Autobiography*, 69). The situation leaves her with anxiety that popularity makes the writer unauthentic.

Success also directed her attention as a writer to the subject of money, on which she comments frequently in *Everybody's Autobiography* and in a series of five articles, published in 1936, for the *Saturday Evening Post*. While this subject inflamed the ideological convictions of Ezra Pound, another expatriate American writer of the period, it amused Stein so much that she was led to make unaccustomed speculations on anthropology and society: "The only difference between man and animals is that men can count. No animals count. And of course the thing they count when they count is money, no animal can count money" (*Everybody's Autobiography*, 118). In her own life, the archetypal first step of an American success story had been long delayed: "I always wanted to have earned my first dollar but I never had" (*Everybody's Autobiography*, 40). In calculated contradiction to the deeds of public benefactors like Benjamin Franklin and philanthropists like Andrew Carnegie, however, Stein argues the virtues of avarice.

Gertrude Stein finds compensation in the irony of her situation: "This extraordinary welcome that I am having does not come from the books of mine that they do understand like the Autobiography but the books of mine that they did not understand" (*Everybody's Autobiography*, 8). She considers such accessibility characteristic of the genre: "Autobiography is easy like it or not autobiography is easy for any one and so this is to be everybody's autobiography" (*Everybody's Autobiography*, 6). These thoughts are later echoed in the memorable prediction by

moving audiovisual image rather than to the pages of a text, its authentic place. This brief talkie in a sense stole from the writer her soul, her voice *within* the text.

The question of identity for Stein could only be answered with assurance in this manner: "Writing belonged to me, there is no doubt about it writing belonged to me. I know writing belongs to me, I am quite certain" (*Everybody's Autobiography*, 15). The statement presents a conjugation of the degrees to which Stein is fully in possession of herself through writing. Stein's autobiographies are accounts for public consumption of an essentially private and textual inquiry into matters of the writer's self.

Montaigne's *Essays*, Rousseau's *Confessions*, Sartre's *Words*

Language and Self

Michel de Montaigne's *Essays* inaugurated a tradition of self-inquiry in French writing that also initiated lasting questions of how language represents experience and individuality. This sixteenth-century book is an epic human document of a man's reflections on his immediate experiences, his reading, his sensations, on history, and on information he receives about politics and new discoveries. Montaigne did not write to record his accomplishments, though they were many, as a memoirist does. Rather, his subject is the characteristics of his heart and mind in all their idiosyncrasies and variety. The self-portrait Montaigne offers through his personal essays is modest in its claims, ironic about the self's importance, and mindful of human mortality. Montaigne portrays his individuality as inseparable from shared human fate.

The precedent set by the *Essays* provoked Jean-Jacques Rousseau two centuries later, in writing his *Confessions*, to aim

I am different myself, or whether I take hold of my subjects in different circumstances and aspects. (3.2, 610–11)[2]

Montaigne thus conceives of his self-portrait not as a static composition but rather as a serial representation. The essay mode is best suited for his communication of the immediate, mutable, and provisional qualities of experience. For Montaigne the mode subsumes in discourse the entire record of a life, the events of which, for another writer, might form the basis for a historical narrative.

Discourse is the medium for Montaigne's exercise of judgment, an activity without intermission in the *Essays*. As we remember from Chapter 1, discourse activates self through first-person forms of address. With the personal essay, Montaigne's innovation is to have made himself so forthrightly the sum and substance of his prose. Montaigne employs the first-person singular to proclaim and to pursue himself as the book's subject and to do so by means of his own subjectivity. One of Montaigne's great achievements in language is to have maintained his degree of self-reference without lapsing into solipsism.

On occasion Montaigne directed his judgment toward other cultures, as in "Of Cannibals." Acting as an anthropologist of New World cultures, Montaigne compares the customs of colonized peoples to those of the French, and he concludes that the designations *savage* and *barbarian* are entirely relative terms, reflective only of European preconceptions toward other cultures. Most often, Montaigne acts as an anthropologist toward himself, as a student of the further reaches of his own habits and values. The method of inquiry is based in his humble, receptive, and open-minded temperament. The method is symbolized in the personal medallion that he designed. Bearing a pair of scales in perfect balance, the medallion was inscribed on one side with "I suspend my judgment" in Greek and on the other with "What do I know?" in French. Reservation and incertitude are two sides of a methodical skepticism that, in time, leads to contradictory perspectives. This outcome leaves him humbly self-aware: "I, who make no other profession, find in me such infinite depth and variety, that what I have learned bears no other fruit than to make me realize how much I still have to learn" (*Essays*, 3.13, 823).

The "passing" of thought is the experience that most often captures Montaigne's interest. His modest ambition in writing the *Essays* is to embody thought in language. He considers the aspiration for knowledge to be a natural human desire, as instinctual as the appetites. In the "hunt for knowledge . . . a spirited mind" does not rest: "its pursuits are boundless and without form; its food is wonder, the chase, ambiguity" (*Essays*, 3.13, 818). Montaigne reasons that thought, like an animal in nature or a bodily organ, is best left to function without restriction. He nonetheless distinguishes the mind as the human faculty of highest order, possessed of a sublime potential for development and refinement through learning.

The *Essays* consistently place high value on a natural style of expression. By naturalness in language, Montaigne means a writing that retains the exercise and effort of thought. Without apology, he characterizes his sentences as loose and disjointed and as lacking formal logic or coherent argument. Gertrude Stein's method of a "moving existing" style in her thought and language is directly analogous to Montaigne's practices as a writer. Montaigne aspires to an appearance of unclothed and unimproved thought in prose: "I would indeed correct an accidental error, and I am full of them, since I run on carelessly. But the imperfections that are ordinary and constant in me it would be treachery to remove" (*Essays*, 3.5, 667). The pact of good faith applies also, then, to the relation between style and self. The primary experience of Montaigne, for the purposes of his book, is writing itself. To be true to life, imperfections are retained in the writing, even while Montaigne engaged in extensive augmentation, rethinking, and revision over his nearly two decades of work on the *Essays*.

In the early essay "Of Prompt or Slow Speech" Montaigne describes his experience of composing in prose: "I will have tossed off some subtle remark as I write. . . . Later I have lost the point so thoroughly that I do not know what I meant; and sometimes a stranger has discovered it before I do. If I erased every passage where this happens to me, there would be nothing left of myself" (*Essays*, 1.10, 27). The correlation of text with self in this statement is complete and unmediated. To make the case for his style, Montaigne perhaps overstates the tendency of his writing to leave himself baffled. In any event, there is room within

emotional nakedness in his self-portrait. He proceeds on the principle that "there is no human heart, however pure, that does not conceal some odious vice" (*Confessions*, 479). In the course of his *Confessions*, Rousseau takes punitive pleasure in revealing himself at his worst in the past. The process of confession gives priority to narrative over discourse in his book.

Rousseau shaped, as did Wordsworth, the widely influential Romantic conception of the child as father to the man. After devoting great attention to events of his childhood and youth, Rousseau pauses to explain his rationale: "Although in certain respects I have been a man since birth, I was for a long time, and still am, a child in many others. I never promised to present the public with a great personage. I promised to depict myself as I am; and to know me in my later years it is necessary to have known me well in my youth" (*Confessions*, 169). The ideas and impressions of life's first phase form "the original set" and "the prime causes" of all subsequent experience for him (*Confessions*, 169).

Narrative in the *Confessions* starts from a point of romantic agony: "I was born, a poor and sickly child, and cost my mother her life. So my birth was the first of my misfortunes" (*Confessions*, 19). The newborn was not only the death of his mother; Rousseau was himself "almost born dead" (*Confessions*, 336). His legacy at birth was "but one, a sensitive heart," which remains the prime mover through the duration of his long narrative (*Confessions*, 19). This prime cause is subject, however, to inversions such as that between innocence and perverse desire. Away at boarding school at age eight, Rousseau's "strongest desire was to be loved" (*Confessions*, 25). Nonetheless, when he received corporal punishment at the hands of the school mistress he experienced unexpected gratification: "This punishment increased my affection for the inflicter. It required all the strength of my devotion and all my natural gentleness to prevent my deliberately earning another beating; I had discovered in the shame and pain of the punishment an admixture of sensuality which had left me rather eager than otherwise for a repetition" (*Confessions*, 25).

Rousseau confesses that this experience cast the mold of "my tastes and desires, my passions, my very self for the rest of my life" (*Confessions*, 26). While it did not cost him his innocence, the experience irreparably complicated his natural purity. The later affairs with Mme de Larnage and Mme de Warens represent the two extremes of mature passion for Rousseau. With Mme de Larnage, Rousseau experienced a fulfillment "pure and sharp and without any alloy of pain" that was unprecedented (*Confessions*, 240). He describes it as the uncommon experience of being fully in possession of his natural, best self. But such fulfillment does not qualify as love for Rousseau. An alloy of pain is found in his relationship with Mme de Warens, or "Mamma," as he affectionately called her: "With Mamma my pleasure was always troubled by a feeling of sadness, by a secret oppression at the heart that I had difficulty in overcoming; instead of congratulating myself upon possessing her, I would reproach myself for degrading her" (*Confessions*, 241). Rousseau confesses to only one "true love" in life, for Mme d'Houdetot, though the passion was not mutual and was never fulfilled in sensuality (*Confessions*, 241). Without consummation, the love for Mme d'Houdetot allowed him to maintain ideals uncompromised by physical passion or perversion, and thus Rousseau achieved romantic fulfillment.

Another pattern of inversion established for Rousseau in youth is one between his own victimization and his urge to betray and to humiliate others. While still in boarding school, Rousseau was wrongly accused for damaging the school mistress's hair comb and then was unjustly punished by his uncle. Rousseau proclaims that the experience forged in him a resolute compassion: "My blood boils at the sight or the tale of any injustice, whoever may be the sufferer and wherever it may have taken place, in just the same way as if I myself were its victim" (*Confessions*, 30). In service to Mme de Vercellis as valet at age sixteen, however, Rousseau stole a decorative ribbon and charged the household cook, an innocent girl, with the theft. Since the ribbon was found in his possession, the two of them were dismissed from the household.

Rousseau claims that the betrayal has so lastingly seared his conscience that it has "greatly contributed to my resolution of writing these *Confessions*" (*Confessions*, 88). He characterizes the act as an inoculation that has preserved his original purity: "I have derived some benefit from the terrible impression left with me by the sole offense I have committed. For it has secured me for the rest of my life against any act that might prove criminal in its results" (*Confessions*, 89). The rationalization made here resembles Benjamin Franklin's explanation of how the "Errata" and "Faults" of his youth served to preserve him from worse errors in

sity of seeking a livelihood forces them apart. It is neither hunger nor thirst but love, hatred, pity, anger, which drew from them the first words."[7] Poetry was the original type of language. Its original purposes were for essential human acts such as "moving a young heart, or repelling an unjust aggressor" (*Languages*, 12). Rousseau contends that the basis for institutions was the same as that for the arts in the earliest societies, that "the first laws were sung" (*Languages*, 51).

Logic, exposition, and argument are much later developments and belong to the domain of writing. The advancement of civilization through force and trade brought great loss to the natural music and poetry once inherent in language. With the development of commerce and political domination, language became debased. The consolidation of learning into institutions contributed to the process: "The study of philosophy and the progress of reason, while having perfected grammar, deprive language of its vital, passionate quality, which made it so singable" (*Languages*, 68). The same claim of fundamental degeneration in human culture is made by Claude Lévi-Strauss in *Tristes Tropiques* (1955), the autobiography of his life as an anthropologist.

The ontogeny narrated in the *Confessions* recapitulates in some measure the anthropogeny outlined in the *Essay on the Origin of Languages*. Humanity evolved through savage and barbaric stages before establishing the pastoral societies that made speech possible. Compassion and human unity emerge along with speech at the pastoral stage: "We develop social feeling only as we become enlightened. Although pity is native to the human heart, it would remain eternally quiescent unless it were activated by imagination" (*Languages*, 32). The childhood Rousseau portrays in his *Confessions* is endowed with serenity, pure happiness, and instinctive virtue. Circumstances allowed Rousseau the freedom to educate his own imagination and passions: "I felt before I thought: which is the common lot of man, though more pronounced in my case than in another's" (*Confessions*, 19).

The child attained literacy through the novels his mother had left after her death. Initially, his father recited from them; then at age five or six Rousseau began to decipher their language by himself. Through this process, Rousseau attains the pastoral stage: "It is from my earliest reading that I date the unbroken consciousness of my own existence. . . . I had no idea of the facts, but I was already familiar with every feeling. I had grasped nothing; I had sensed everything" (*Confessions*, 19–20). Under the benevolent guidance of his father, his reading expanded to include history and myth. The material and their discussions over it instilled in Rousseau a republican spirit and an antipathy to injustice.

The *Confessions* narrates the progressive separation of Rousseau from the kind of social circumstances that nourish humanity's inherent virtues. His impulsive decision in 1749 to enter an essay competition sponsored by the Dijon Academy marks the point of no return in this separation: "All the rest of my life and of my misfortunes followed inevitably as a result of that moment's madness" (*Confessions*, 328). With the decision he crosses a threshold into public life as a man of letters. From that point forward commerce and politics, to which a professional writer must inevitably submit, threaten Rousseau's natural genius and eloquence. As Rousseau gains greater recognition as a writer, literary reputation leads him unsuspectingly into the "barbaric" worlds of the *salon* and the academy. Thus, when Rousseau is elevated to celebrity status he experiences a degree of loss to his authentic self. Gertrude Stein acknowledges a similar cost of celebrity.

Rousseau is insistent that the *Confessions* is not intended as an *apology*, in the generic sense of that term. Nevertheless, the book is meant to restore his original innocence. Speech, not writing, is the mode of language most true to the self. His first act of confession took place in childhood in the form of conversation with a girl of the same age. It involved his sensual taste for punishment, a matter that he confesses only once again, in his book. The ease and effectiveness of his confession in conversation on that occasion were soon lost, along with the untroubled innocence of childhood. Apprenticed in adolescence to an engraver, his master's tyranny drove Rousseau "to covet in silence, to conceal, to dissimulate, to lie" (*Confessions*, 40–41). Each of these corruptions to his natural character debases the faculty of speech.

In many of the social and amorous situations of adult life, Rousseau describes himself as awkward and inappropriate in the conversation he makes or as at a total loss for words. True to other inversions in his experience, the eloquence and authenticity attributed to speech can be approximated by Rousseau only

future penetrates to the heart of each one as a real motivation for his behavior."[11] For his autobiography, therefore, childhood can only be represented in terms of the writer and intellectual Sartre becomes.

Conditions of negation defined Sartre's being in early life: "*I was not* substantial or permanent, *I was not* the future continuer of my father's work, *I was not* necessary" (*Words*, 55). His identity is a construct and project left to the culture that surrounded him. The earliest influences came from popular culture, particularly from motion pictures, whose birth was nearly contemporary with his own: "This new art was mine, just as it was everyone else's. We had the same mental age: I was seven and knew how to read; it was twelve and did not know how to talk (*Words*, 77). In play, the child recreated the environment of the silent movie theater: "I decided to lose the power of speech and to live in music. . . . I became then and there the flat image of the musketeer" (*Words*, 79). As his mother performed classical music on the piano for her own pleasure, the child acted out elaborate scenarios in the library, responding to the music as accompaniment to his screen adventures.

Ironically, language played a secondary role in the formation of his self-image. The turning point in childhood, from reading to writing, is summarized as the adoption of "a new imposture" (*Words*, 85). Writing began at age seven in the form of letters in verse to his grandfather. The new activity made him newly conscious that playacting his own adventure stories had been a "double imposture: I was pretending to be an actor who was pretending to be a hero" (*Words*, 87).[12] But the child seated precociously at a writing desk could not restrain himself from committing further impostures: "I would pucker my brow, assume a moonstruck expression, so as to feel I was a *writer*. I loved plagiarism" (*Words*, 88).

French Autobiography and Philosophical Inquiry

Over the course of more than two decades, Sartre developed a comprehensive *biographical* method to render his philosophical views on self—a first book on Charles Baudelaire (1947), followed by a study on Jean Genet (1952), and culminated in the monumental work on Gustave Flaubert (1971). One conclusion

Sartre reached is summarized in the study on Flaubert: "A man is never an individual; it would be more fitting to call him a *universal singular*. Summed up and for this reason universalized by his epoch, he in turn resumes it by reproducing himself in it as singularity."[13] A similar rationale governs the representation of self in *The Words*, but it is given form by Sartre as a novelist rather than as a philosopher. Presented by his family with a composition book and a bottle of purple ink, he inscribed the cover "Novel Notebook" and began to write. By age nine he had completed the initial work in his career: "With my first novel I knew that a child had got into a hall of mirrors . . . and if I said 'I,' that meant 'I who write'" (*Words*, 95). His identity now belonged with the universality that bourgeois culture presumes. The passion to write involved a denial of ordinary, simply individual, experience.

The writing life is delineated in *The Words* as paradoxical in its inception, as "the realization of the imaginary" (*Words*, 88). Sartre portrays a child who imagines future fame for the writer that comes at the cost of a life spent in solitude and emotional deprivation. He offers the portrait as a wish fulfillment that patently conforms to bourgeois myths of the artist as a lonely genius. The projected future also converts present experience into a form of nonexistence: "I chose as my future the past of a great immortal and I tried to live backwards. I became completely posthumous" (*Words*, 124). This last paradox conveys a goal of liberation that Sartre sought as a writer in the face of bourgeois values. In his manifesto *What is Literature?* (1947), Sartre formulates the goal as follows: "In a society which insists upon production and restricts consumption to what is strictly necessary, the work of literature is evidently gratuitous. . . . This gratuity, far from grieving us, is our pride, and we know that it is the image of freedom."[14]

The Words modifies the *cogito* of Western philosophy, the Cartesian principle "I think, therefore I am." Unable to recall any of the contents in his first compositions, Sartre thinks of them as activity without substance or purpose other than itself. Nonetheless, the activity engendered his identity: "I was born of writing" (*Words*, 95). Writing for Sartre is not a matter of a corrupted language as distinct from original, pure speech. Language in all forms is artifice. And identity is founded upon such artifice: "By writing I was existing, . . . but I existed only in order to write" (*Words*, 95).

Jean Genet, *The Thief's Journal*, and Violette Leduc, *La Bâtarde*

Autobiography and *L'Écrivain Maudit*

In French literature there is a well-established tradition of genius marginal to society or outcast from it. The tradition is known by the term *poète maudit*, accursed or damned poet. An early figure in the tradition is François Villon, considered one of the great French writers of the late Middle Ages and one of the finest lyric poets in the language. The events of his life document a criminal history. Born in 1431, Villon developed ties with the underworld of Paris in his student years. His livelihood often derived from begging or robbery. During a brawl, he killed a priest. In the course of his life, Villon was imprisoned or sent into exile a number of times. Subsequent to the commutation in 1463 of a death sentence against him, Villon disappeared during exile; the date and circumstances of his death remain unknown.

The *poète maudit* was celebrated in the nineteenth century, particularly by writers inspired by the modern city, such as

raphy asserts his poverty, vagrancy, homosexuality, and criminal activities as inspirations to his writing. There is no guilty conscience or compulsion to confess in the book, nor any claim that society has victimized him.

The Thief's Journal narrates the existential desideratum of Genet's life, that is, its willed project and future: "Toward what is known as evil, I lovingly pursued an adventure which led me to prison" (*Journal*, 9). In a preface to the book, Sartre separates Genet from Montaigne and the conventions of self-study. Sartre advises the reader to respond to the book as "a sacred cosmogony; . . . you think he is relating *facts* and suddenly you realize he is describing rites" (*Journal*, 8–9). Genet certifies this directive, terming the *Journal* an intimate mythology rather than a conventional autobiography: "Not my life, but the interpretation of it. It is what language offers me to evoke it, to talk about it, to render it. To achieve my legend" (*Journal*, 205).

The book's language is primarily a medium for poetry and fantasy rather than for history. Genet offers its imagery as the measure of his passions and imagination: "I speak of this period with emotion, and I magnify it, but if glamorous words, I mean words charged in my mind with more glamour than meaning, occur to me, they do so perhaps because the poverty they express, which was mine too, is likewise a source of wonder" (*Journal*, 58–59). The splendor and nobility with which Genet endows experience require, for their meaning, a context of misery and deprivation.

Genet forewarns readers that he employs language in paradoxical and dialectical constructs: "This kind of definition—by so many opposing examples— . . . shows you that I shall not make use of words the better to depict an event or its hero, but so that they may tell you something about myself" (*Journal*, 16). His method of representation is one of mirroring, which replicates a likeness while reversing its lateral orientation. Dialectical oppositions operate perpetually in his forbidden universe.[2] Experience that lacerates his emotions are the means "by which beauty was revealed" (*Journal*, 18). Abjection and shame are the starting point for a pilgrimage toward sanctity. Abasement contains the sublime within it. An act of betrayal brings joy to the traitor. Anguish becomes a state of radiance.

Genet's profane testament renames and ritualizes experience that originally brought degradation, physical humiliation, or fear. The process is reflected in complaints attributed to a transvestite prostitute as he selects articles from his wardrobe in preparation for the evening clientele: "I feel as if I were going into a vestry to get ready to conduct a funeral. They've got a priestish smell. Like incense. Like urine. Look at them hanging! I wonder how I manage to get into those damned sausage skins" (*Journal*, 66). Within Genet's creation, the accursed and the sacred are inseparable. His many misfortunes are greeted as a sign of grace.

Raging hatred accompanies sexual consummation. Violence flowers in the fights common to the city districts Genet frequents: "It was the younger who fell, his temple smashed by the iron fist of the other, who watched the blood flow and become a tuft of primroses" (*Journal*, 210). The first grand passion in Genet's life is conceived in the midst of events that involve the fatal stabbing of a gypsy, an act committed by his companion Pépé: "Pépé had disappeared, but when, turning my eyes away from the corpse, I looked up, there, gazing at it with a faint smile, was Stilitano. The sun was about to set. The dead man and the handsomest of humans seemed to me merged in the same golden dust. . . . At the same moment I came to know death and love" (*Journal*, 39). The fascination Stilitano holds for Genet dwells in his untouchable mastery, to which the acolyte in love and crime dutifully submits.

The right hand of this professional criminal had been amputated at the wrist. Stilitano adopts the adoring young man as an accomplice and introduces Genet around the quarter as "his right arm." The role is a source of pride for Genet: "I was the one who took the place of the strongest limb" (*Journal*, 43–44). In portraying himself as the surrogate for the missing limb, Genet creates an ideal self that possesses the same powers he attributes to the manhood concealed in Stilitano's pants: "Unable to see it, I invented the biggest and loveliest prick in the world. I endowed it with qualities: heavy, strong and nervous, sober, with a tendency toward pride and yet serene" (*Journal*, 43). His fantasy is resolutely free of the Freudian determinism that diagnoses homosexual desire as a pathology.

Vagabondage also defines his existence and identity in the years recounted in *The Thief's Journal*. In his wanderings, Genet traversed much of western, central, and Mediterranean Europe. The crossing into a new country is an encounter with "the interior of an image" rather than a cultural or political transition (*Journal*, 49). The circumstances of entrance into a new country often entailed his expulsion from a neighboring one. Genet adopts a rootless, transient state of being as his *place* in life.

Often it was necessary for Genet to fake or forge the documents necessary for transit at national borders. The fact of his false identity papers is a suitable metaphor for the conditions of his life. Fakery is a form of misdeed that particularly appeals to Genet. He praises the extravagant self-dramatization of able-bodied beggars who claim to be impaired. He is charmed by fakery obvious in its falsehood, as found among manly transvestites. On one occasion, Stilitano claims to have boldly stolen a motorcycle from a uniformed police officer. When it turns out that the officer conspired with Stilitano in the theft, Genet is not disillusioned: "A discovery of this kind ought to have estranged me from him; it made him dearer to me. I was in love with a fake hoodlum who was in cahoots with a cop. As a team, they were a traitor and an impostor" (*Journal*, 183).

Later, as a test of loyalty, Stilitano proposes the robbery of a mutual friend. Genet agrees to the plan on the basis of its perverse and beautiful logic: "The idea of betraying Armand set me aglow. I feared and loved him too much not to want to deceive and betray and rob him. I sensed the anxious pleasure that goes with sacrilege" (*Journal*, 261). In all cases, the autobiography exalts theft as an enterprise of imagination, as an act of poetry. A burglary entails archetypal experience: "I am steeped in an idea of property while I loot property. I recreate the absent proprietor. He lives, not facing me, but about me. He is a fluid element which I breathe, which enters me, which inflates my lungs" (*Journal*, 155–56). The last details describe, in a literal sense of the term, an *inspired* state.

Theft itself is robbed of meaning, however, when Genet crosses the border into Nazi Germany. There, he is inhibited in the pursuit of crime, which elsewhere has an allure of heroism: "'It's a race of thieves,' I thought to myself. 'If I steal here, I perform no singular deed that might fulfill me. I obey the customary order; I do not destroy it. I am not committing evil. I am not upsetting anything. The outrageous is impossible. I'm stealing in the void'" (*Journal*, 123). The act would lack the degree of existential negation necessary to Genet's sense of identity. Under Hitler, German authority "succeeded in being both Police and Crime" in a synthesis so complete that any oppositional, marginal position is nullified (*Journal*, 189).

In the other countries of Europe, Genet can depend upon a quality of universality in the company of petty criminals, prostitutes, gypsies, and other outcasts. The many thieves of his acquaintance comprise a fraternity: "These fellows, scattered all over France, and sometimes in foreign countries, are a comfort to me, even though I may not see them often. It makes me feel calm and glad to know they are alive, active and handsome, lurking in the shadow" (*Journal*, 250–51). Genet also experiences fellowship in humiliation. One instance is in the company of Barcelona's beggars when they pose for the cameras of tourists, ashore for a few hours from the ocean liners: "Foreigners in this country, wearing fine gabardines, rich, they recognized their inherent right to find these archipelagoes of poverty picturesque. . . . With an excess of servility, the beggars arranged themselves in the filthiest spots, disdainful of the slightest precaution for their own person" (*Journal*, 164, 166).

The Past as Pre-Text

Two French criminal records photographs of himself—one taken at age sixteen, the other at thirty—lead Genet into reflection upon his perception of the world and the world's perception of him in these two periods of life. In the photograph from his youth he finds purity and pathos in the sad, blasé expression on his face. The adult autobiographer knows himself to have been insolent and brazen at that age. But at twilight, in weariness, the adolescent would become "aware of my utter solitude" (*Journal*, 85). The identity photograph captures a sense of salvation from that solitude: "Prison offered me the first consolation, the first peace, the first friendly fellowship: I experienced them in the realm of foulness" (*Journal*, 85).[3] The face of the thirty-year-old in the second photograph is hardened, bitter, and mean. Among the features of this hoodlum, a suggestion of gentleness is none-theless detectable in the eyes.

The hint of gentleness is a window to a soul of devotion and compassion, qualities that Genet characterizes in feminine terms: "I pursued . . . my identification with the handsomest and most unfortunate criminals. I wanted to be the young prostitute who accompanies her lover to Siberia or the one who survives him, not in order to avenge him, but to mourn him and magnify his memory" (*Journal*, 86). Genet thus makes a claim for an essential purity of heart. He does not sentimentalize, however, the trans-formation of his personality captured in the contrasts between the two photographs. Rather than treat the transformation as a matter of lost innocence or one of his victimization by society, Genet sees in it the fulfillment of a self-determined providence: "The uncertainty of my origin allowed me to interpret it. I added to it the peculiarity of my misfortunes. Abandoned by my family, I already felt it was natural to aggravate this condition by a pref-erence for boys, and this preference by theft, and theft by crime or a complacent attitude in regard to crime. I thus resolutely rejected a world which had rejected me. This almost gleeful rushing into the most humiliating situations is perhaps still moti-vated by my childhood imagination" (*Journal*, 86–87).

Genet determines an incontestable origin for himself and con-sciously creates his destiny when, at age sixteen, he undertakes "a rigorous discipline" in his relationship with social authorities: "to every charge brought against me, unjust though it may be, from the bottom of my heart I shall answer yes. Hardly had I uttered the word—or the phrase signifying it—than I felt within me the need to become what I had been accused of being. I was sixteen years old. The reader has understood: I kept no place in my heart where the feeling of my innocence might take shelter. I owned to being the coward, traitor, thief and fairy they saw in me" (*Journal*, 175–76). In his study on Genet, Sartre identifies this experience as the point of conception in Genet's project of exis-tential identity.[4]

His acts of existential assertion are predicated on a mirroring of the names with which society officially condemns him. For Genet, language is the inner sanctum of an intimate mythology. It is a repository for ritual, often sacred, meanings: "If I examine my work, I now perceive in it, patiently pursued, a will to rehabilitate persons, objects and feelings reputedly vile. . . . I was not trying to make excuses for them. Nor to justify them. I wanted them to have the right to the honors of the Name" (*Journal*, 109). The name of an ideal or of a desired quality, like that of a loved person, is a form of effigy magic: "Though saintliness is my goal, I cannot tell what it is. My point of departure is the word itself, which indicates the state closest to moral perfection. Of which I know nothing, save that without it my life would be in vain. Unable to give a definition of saintliness—no more than I can of beauty—I want at every minute to create it" (*Journal*, 208–9). Existential self-creation in Genet's writing can thus be said to take place in name only.

Genet's autobiographical film *Un Chant d'amour* (1950) incorporates imagery from a poem of the same title, which was published in 1948. This silent film in black and white, with a running time of twenty-five minutes, was banned by censors for two decades on the grounds of its explicit homoerotic content. The film lyrically presents a repertoire of images, gestures, and fantasies representative of Genet's intimate imagination. (The recreation of a personal image repertory also has a strong tradition since the 1950s within American independent cinema, in the autobiographical work of filmmakers such as Kenneth Anger, Stan Brakhage, and Jonas Mekas.) Set principally in a prison environment, *Un Chant d'amour* depicts the interlocking desires of two inmates and a guard. The love of one prisoner for the other inmate, who is inexperienced and reluctant in such male romance, exhibits a freedom unknown to the guard, who is captive of his own compulsive voyeurism. The purity of the inmates in their erotic activities remains uncorrupted when the guard takes punitive measures against them. Prominent among the film's images of passion is a garland of flowers, seen against the iron of prison bars and the stone walls of the cells.

In composing *The Thief's Journal*, Genet is acutely conscious of the narrative difficulties in autobiography of recapturing the past: "It is not a quest of time gone by, but a work of art whose pretext-subject is my former life. It will be a present fixed with the help of the past, and not vice versa. Let the reader therefore understand that the facts were what I say they were, but the interpretation that I give them is what I am—now" (*Journal*, 71). This statement of purpose reiterates the interdependence between narrative and discourse characteristic of the genre. With narrative perspective lines drawn from a point of discourse, from a center in the writer's imagination, *The Thief's Journal* treats the past as a *pre-text* for the present. In other words, the autobiography views the past as a form of writing and imagery that is to be now reworked and reanimated. Genet refers to himself as a "repository" for the data of experience (*Journal*, 100). Truth is not a matter of fidelity to that data but is rather one of fidelity to the passions he experiences in regard to them as he writes.

The past eludes recreation in its own right, but the writer can create the intangibles of experience through the names he bestows upon the past. Genet explains his adoration for other young men in prison as a poetic act: "I have forgotten those boys: all that remains of them is the attribute which I have sung, and that is what will glow in my books with a brilliance equal to pride, heroism and boldness" (*Journal*, 109). The experiences that imagination preserves constitute an "ideal presence" out of which Genet composes his text of autobiography: "I undertook, with a baroque intention, to cite a few, pretending to omit those—the first which make up the apparent texture of my life—which are the knots of the glistening thread. If France is an emotion communicated from artist to artist—a relay of neurons, so to speak—then to the very end I am only a string of tinglings" (*Journal*, 117–18). While material from his early life may be left out of the narrative, the omission is only a "pretense" because the writer's discursive present takes form through such material.

To explain the relationship through writing to his past, Genet returns to the idea of a pre-text: "I refuse to live for any other end than the very one which I found to contain the first misfortune: that my life must be a legend, in other words, legible, and the reading of it must give birth to a certain new emotion which I call poetry. I am no longer anything, only a pretext" (*Journal*, 119). Public welfare bureaucrats had consigned Genet to the orphanage and then to a foster family. Social authorities sentenced him to a succession of reformatories and penitentiaries. The criminal system documented his physical appearance with photographs for its files and an "anthropometric" identity card. Against the public record of him as an incorrigible criminal and a social outcast, Genet asserts an identity through writing that revives the margins of freedom in his existence as a vagabond, prisoner, and homosexual.

Leduc: An Identity as a Bastard

Violette Leduc in *La Bâtarde* (1964) treats as essential to identity her existence as the illegitimate daughter of a provincial bourgeois who refused to acknowledge her as his child. With the opening words to her autobiography, Leduc promises an unheroic narrative: "My case is not unique: I am afraid of dying and distressed at being in this world. I haven't worked, I haven't studied. I have wept, I have cried out in protest. These tears and cries have taken up a great deal of my time. . . . There is no sustenance in the past. I shall depart as I arrived. Intact, loaded down, with the defects that have tormented me."[5] Suffering and failure are given meaning, however, insofar as they serve the present purposes of writing. With surprising frequency in *La Bâtarde*, Leduc chronicles the composition of her autobiography with precise, dated references to the circumstances in which incidents are remembered and in which she writes them down or rereads her text. Like Genet, Leduc maintains a dialogue with her past in the course of narrating it. The discourse in *La Bâtarde* extends from 1958 to 1963, the narrative from 1907 to 1944.

The autobiographer in the present remains nevertheless bound to her past. Leduc creates a text in the context of birth ties to her mother and of estrangement, by birth, from her father. Denied both patronymic and patrimony, Leduc bears the maiden name of her mother, Berthe Leduc. An irony in the bourgeois conventions of a respectable woman's "maiden name" resonates in the account of her mother's service to a family of substantial means in northern France. A maidservant in the household, her mother became the lover of André, an indulged and sickly son. With the news of her pregnancy, André begged Berthe to leave town so as not to implicate him, which she did out of loyalty: "My mother loved him. I can't deny it. How did she love him? Courageously, fiercely, wildly. It was the love of a lifetime, it was a victim's march to the sacrifice. I forgive him, she says again. He was sick, he depended on his parents, he was afraid of his father. . . . His soul was less refined. Cowardly, lazy, good for nothing. My mirror, Mother, my mirror. No, I want no part of you, I reject my heredity" (*Bâtarde*, 9). But her bastard heritage is inescapable. Both parent figures mirror her. Leduc's self-image is poised between her mother's suffering presence and power and her father's absence and betrayal. Asked on the school playground

115

who her parents are, the child answers in confusion and shame: "My mother is my father" (*Bâtarde*, 37).

Her self-representation as ugly, degraded, and superfluous is a consequence of her scandalous existence. Though well cared for in childhood by her mother, Leduc bastardizes the account of this attention to appearances: "I must wear a medallion on a slim gold chain, embroidered dresses and long pantalettes, I must have a fair skin and silky hair in order to compete with the rich children in the town. . . . In our room: near-destitution—my chamber pot becomes a salad bowl at the beginning of every meal" (*Bâtarde*, 12). Leduc holds her maternal grandmother Fidéline innocent of these household duplicities and remains faithful to her memory: "Ageless Fidéline, without a woman's face and body, Fidéline my slow priest, I shall always be betrothed to you. Every night was a wedding night when I nested in the hollow of your neck" (*Bâtarde*, 17).[6] The imagery here symbolizes the devotion of a virgin bride to her deity.

Leduc recounts a childhood of illnesses, mishaps, accidents, and injuries, and in these experiences she fulfills the legacy of her ill-fated, tubercular father. He is further mirrored in her mother's warnings against the treachery of men, delivered to Violette in childhood: "Each morning she made me a terrible gift: the gift of suspicion and mistrust. All men were swine, men had no hearts. She stared at me with such intensity as she made this statement that I would wonder whether perhaps I wasn't a man. There wasn't a single one among them to redeem the race as a whole" (*Bâtarde*, 25). The wrongs that Berthe suffered from André are the symbolic patrimony Violette shall receive. Berthe further imposes them upon her daughter by putting Violette into the position of his accomplice.

Loves and Letters

Her grandmother Fidéline died when Violette was nine years old, and her mother married by the time Violette reached age thirteen. Between these two events, Leduc had her first experience of adolescent sexuality with a boy. Once he finished satisfying himself against her body, the boy murmured "I've married you" (*Bâtarde*, 32). From that moment onward he ignored her entirely. The experience left Violette in tears, but it made no emotional sense to her. The indifference of the male world soon becomes personified in her remote and silent stepfather. Life in his home compounds her sense of ugliness and futility to the point where she fantasizes a new version of beauty and the beast: "When would I meet an ogre? I would love him. I would hold up a mirror in front of him, I would say: I can see two roses in the mirror. Look, please look: one is you, the other is me" (*Bâtarde*, 50). At age seventeen, she discovers fulfillment and transcendence in her first romantic relationship, with Isabelle, a fellow student at boarding school.

The love between Isabelle and Violette is tested when Isabelle graduates and summer comes. After her return to school alone, Violette conceives and fulfills a new passion, with the music teacher Hermine. As soon as the school's administrator learns of their relationship, however, Hermine is dismissed. In anguish, Violette dedicates herself to the vision of Greek tragedy and the Stoic ideas she has discovered in the classroom. Reading becomes a profound experience: "The eternity of God was now the eternity to be found in the simplicity of a text" (*Bâtarde*, 105). Inspired by moral philosophy, she formulates a personal code that contains a strong existential overtone: "I shall be the anvil on which I forge my own sorrow" (*Bâtarde*, 105). Some months later, when love letters from Hermine are discovered, Violette is expelled from the school.

The intimate letter held, as a literary form, particular powers for Leduc, much as the diary form held for woman writers like Mary Chesnut and Anaïs Nin. It offers Leduc a degree of directness and immediacy and a context of private, shared communication that gratifies the ideal self that she desires: "Living as I did for the letters I wrote at night, the letters I always carried with me, the letters I was constantly expecting, my inner pretensions increased in proportion to my feelings" (*Bâtarde*, 105). On several occasions her autobiography directly addresses the individual reader. The book's last paragraph begins: "August 22, 1963. This August day, reader, is a rose window glowing with heat. I make you a gift of it, it is yours" (*Bâtarde*, 488). Compressed into three lines is a personal letter, inclusive of a complimentary close.

Having failed the oral part of her *baccalauréat* examination, Leduc worked in Paris during the late 1920s in secretarial jobs for a publishing house and a film company. Her relationship with Hermine progressed to the stage where they established a domestic life together. For a time, Leduc cultivated a masculine style in her appearance: "I had hardened the baroque features of my face by razor-cutting my hair short above the temples; I wanted to be a hard focus of attention" (*Bâtarde*, 163–64). At the same time, Hermine admired the standard of feminine beauty promoted in high-fashion magazines. With Hermine's collaboration, Leduc begins to imitate these images of beauty. In elaborate make-up and dressed in current fashion, Leduc self-consciously enters a realm of luxury and coquetry. She takes afternoon walks along Paris boulevards to see what effect on men she has as an object of desire. With a conspiratorial pleasure, she reports to Hermine the results of these seductive expeditions. Though there is emotional satisfaction in the experience, Leduc intellectually evaluates her emulation of bourgeois conventions of femininity as a form of prostitution.

Over these same years, Violette formed a deep emotional bond with Gabriel Mercier. They met in 1926 by chance, during a matinee at a Paris movie theater. A few years older than Leduc, Mercier was employed in the capital as a purchasing agent for a commercial firm in the provincial town Clermont. In the first phase of their relationship, which started while Leduc was still a *lycée* student, she enjoyed new feelings of independence in the books and ideas they shared. During this phase, Leduc satisfies a compulsion to conceal her unconsummated love for Gabriel from her lover Hermine. In the frustration of her carnal desires for Gabriel, Leduc takes pleasure in an arduous, intimate confession—now given to the reader, at the time voiced only in her thoughts and withheld from Hermine.

After Gabriel becomes known to Hermine, a triangular relationship forms that repeats the earlier patterns of the Violette-Isabelle-Hermine relationship. To her own mind, the basis for this emotional archetype was set by the circumstances of her bastard existence. She is destined to be bound anxiously close with the available parent (partner) in alliance against the absent parent (partner). The effects of such a symbiotic relationship between child and mother are summarized in the title to her first book, *L'Asphyxie* (1946), which renders an account of those years. In mature relationships the bond is subject to sudden reversals, with Violette betraying her partner for the third person or with Violette becoming the victim of their alliance and betrayal.

Leduc asserts her independence from Hermine by coercing her to engage in an act of love together for the gratification of a male voyeur. This carnal experience eventually ruins their love. Though she had desired autonomy, Leduc is thrown into despair when Hermine leaves her some months later. The sequence of events fulfills the destiny of suffering she had predicted for herself. Though he is initially attentive and supportive, Gabriel grows aloof, enigmatic, and ultimately cruel in his relations with Leduc. Hermine had provided a stimulus to their love. In her absence, the shared passion between Violette and Gabriel dissipates. Though intermittent, their involvement nevertheless continues during the 1930s.

An Identity as a Writer

In the midst of war hysteria at the end of the decade, Gabriel and Violette agree to marry. She considers her decision a heroic, sacrificial act: "I would have gone to the scaffold to marry him" (*Bâtarde*, 300). The emotional union of husband and wife remains unconsummated, however, and Leduc recognizes that she has sacrificed her peace of mind. In an effort to preserve her integrity, Leduc continues to use her unmarried name in social and professional situations. By this time she has also formed an emotional attachment to Maurice Sachs, a man even more problematic than her husband. An uninhibited homosexual, Sachs cultivated a reputation among Paris intellectuals and artists for his dishonesty and self-indulgence.

This condescending, opinionated, and unpredictable man became a mentor to Leduc. He promoted the start of her writing career by putting Leduc in contact with editors who would assign her journal and magazine pieces. Leduc ironically estimates what success she had as a writer during the war years as a matter of a bastard's good luck: "It was only in a Paris stripped of all its really able people that I, an office mediocrity, was able to write editorials for the ladies and young girls who needed something to read in the Métro" (*Bâtarde*, 348). Regardless of the circumstances, she was determined that all her writing was to be done in the person of an unmarried woman, Mlle Violette Leduc: "Invincible celibacy, I had hidden my wedding ring in my handbag before going into the magazine office. . . . A self-sufficient woman must be single, I had told myself in the waiting room. . . . I had conceived a longing for a double life" (*Bâtarde*, 319). Her writing, and its often antagonistic muse Maurice Sachs, will function in her marriage as the archetypal third party.

After leaving occupied Paris for a village in Normandy, Leduc found a new vocation in the black market that controlled the supply of food from the countryside to the city. In the matter of war profiteering, Maurice Sachs functioned again as her mentor. At the start of the war, Sachs had exploited Jewish families who hired his services for safe passage to the unoccupied zone. In 1942 Sachs and Leduc rented rooms in a village house and managed an illegal trade in food supplies. Their physical proximity made her attachment to Sachs a greater torment. She terms her unfulfilled desires for this man—who asserted that his homosexuality put him beyond the reach of any woman—"a passport to the impossible" (*Bâtarde*, 271).

During the war, she discovers within herself a genius for accumulation and commerce: "I became the slave of my baskets. But the slavery was good for me. My health became a thing of iron in the forge of my endurance, my perseverance, my dishonesty. Bent beneath the weight of my baskets, that is how I explored the resources that lay inside myself" (*Bâtarde*, 446). This self-assessment acknowledges the unheroic aspects of her newly gained power. It is a minor reflection of the wartime corruption in which Maurice Sachs engaged. In about 1944 Sachs relocated to Germany under mysterious circumstances; after 1945 he was not heard from again. Seemingly in emulation of him, on the eve of the Allied liberation of France, Leduc betrayed to police the farmers with whom she had traded so profitably.

During their time together in the Normandy village, Sachs composed his autobiography, which was published posthumously under the title *Le Sabbat: souvenirs d'une jeunesse orageuse* (The sabbath: memories of a stormy youth, 1960; published in translation as *Witches' Sabbath*). The first to read his manuscript, Leduc admired its irony and the larger-than-life quality in self-representation: "The style is Maurice making a game out of his difficulties, it is Maurice proving himself stronger than style and bigger than mere literature" (*Bâtarde*, 408). His autobiography possesses a posture and a style that Leduc considered unattainable in her own writing. Leduc began to write directly about herself after Sachs, in exasperation, instructed her to write down all her grievances about the past instead of letting them habitually intrude into their conversations.

As she begins to follow this instruction, Leduc rediscovers a past in her life that offers an alternative to the existential destiny of sorrow: "The pleasure of foreseeing that my grandmother was about to be reborn, that I was going to bring her into the world; the pleasure of foreseeing that I would be the creator of my grandmother whom I adored, of my grandmother who adored me. To write . . . That seemed superfluous to me as I remembered my tenderness for her, her tenderness for me" (*Bâtarde*, 418). In this regard, writing promises to mirror an ideal image, without sinister or perverse reversals in the bond with her grandmother.

Ultimately, however, in accounting for the past Leduc also remains loyal to the betrayals she experienced in childhood. The narrative she composed in this period opens: "My mother never gave me her hand. . . . She always helped me on and off pavements by pinching my frock or coat very lightly at the spot where the armhole provides a grip. It humiliated me."[7] The memory typifies the pattern of denial and estranged attachment in their relationship. These lines immediately captured the interest of Simone de Beauvoir, the important French novelist and social thinker, when she first read them in 1945.

De Beauvoir was working at the time on *The Second Sex* (1949), a cultural and philosophical study of female identity that has had great influence in the women's movement. She became a compassionate and nurturing mentor to Leduc. Their personal and professional relationship is recounted in Leduc's second volume of autobiography, *La Folie en tête* (*Mad in Pursuit*, 1970), which covers events in the period 1944–1954. A third volume, *La Chasse à l'amour* (Hunting for love, 1973), concerns her life in the period 1954–1964, and it was brought to publication by de Beauvoir one year after Leduc's death.

The example of de Beauvoir as a writer provided Leduc an entirely new muse. Upon first holding Simone de Beauvoir's novel *L'Invitée* (The guest, 1943; translated as *She Came to Stay*) in her hands, Leduc had the following reaction: "To say that I was stirred would be inadequate. I read and reread that name, that title: a woman was writing on behalf of millions of other women, as though all women were capable of writing."[8] For her part, in introducing *La Bâtarde*, de Beauvoir adopts the narrative as an archetype of the cultural and psychological circumstances of "the second sex": "Throughout the years of childhood, her mother inspired her with an irremediable sense of guilt: guilt for having been born, for having delicate health, for costing money, for being a woman and therefore condemned to the miseries of the feminine condition" (*Bâtarde*, vi). Her mother's warnings about the opposite sex shape Leduc's initial identification of womanhood as the gender threatened and condemned by the male domain.

De Beauvoir finds that Leduc's account of the painful struggles with her identity and of the often tortured relationships with men fulfills the existential truth that "a life is the reworking of a destiny by freedom" (*Bâtarde*, vi). And she credits Leduc with a sincerity more authentic and penetrating than that traditional to the confession, well beyond the standard of sincerity claimed by Jean-Jacques Rousseau: "She offers no extenuations. Most writers, when they confess to evil thoughts, manage to remove the sting from them by the very frankness of their admissions. She forces us to feel them with all their corrosive bitterness, both in herself and in ourselves. She remains a faithful accomplice to her desires, to her rancor, to her petty traits" (*Bâtarde*, xvii). These qualities in her personality and in her writing create a dynamic and intimate identification between the reader and the autobiographer.

In the opinion of de Beauvoir, that identification takes place at the margins of society, in situations where the social outcast hears maledictions such as "bastard": "All forms of distress find an echo inside her: that of the abandoned, of the lost, of homeless children. . . . Confronted with injustice, she immediately takes the part of the oppressed, of the exploited. They are her brothers, she recognizes herself in them. The people out on the fringes of society seem more real to her than the settled citizens who always behave according to their allotted roles" (*Bâtarde*, xviii). It must also be said, however, that Leduc also acknowledges within herself the black-market exploiter and the potential oppressor.

Through writing, Leduc asserted in adulthood the possibility for a matrilineal integration and coherence, idealized in the memories of her grandmother Fidéline, in a world largely defined by patriarchal authority and antagonism. While such psychological cohesion was never completed or sustained in her personal life, writing at times powerfully served Leduc as a surrogate, as a world elsewhere, for this ideal relationship. Leduc recognizes that this consolation is exceptional and fictional. She devotes her autobiographies to the communication of the raw emotional complexity in a woman's experience.

Simone de Beauvoir's many volumes of autobiography undertake a similar project, but the formative relationship with her mother differs significantly. As recounted in *Memoirs of a Dutiful Daughter* (1958), maternal love gave de Beauvoir in childhood a security of being that sustains her as she matures. Though bound by many bourgeois conventions, her mother possessed a strength of personality and a compassion that enabled the daughter to believe that being female was not a condemnation. This belief became a foundation upon which to base her ultimate independence from masculine dictates. In *A Very Easy Death* (1964), a memoir of the last months in her mother's life, de Beauvoir reflects on the meaning of their relationship.

Culturally, the genre autobiography has performed as an agent of change, independence, and liberation. As society changes, previous cultural boundaries are crossed or altered, and cultural margins are redefined. The variety in ethnic and social experiences represented through autobiography illuminates, enlarges, and democratizes a nation's traditional, mainstream culture. Within the past three decades in the United States, for example, many works of autobiography have contributed to new social understanding. The genre is important to contemporary Native American writing, as in N. Scott Momaday's *The Way to Rainy Mountain* (1969) and *The Names: A Memoir* (1976), which tell equally of individual experience and of the Kiowa people. On both individual and social levels, Maxine Hong Kingston conveys Asian-American experience, and its specific meaning for women, in *The Woman Warrior: Memoirs of a Girlhood among Ghosts* (1976) and *China Men* (1980). Homosexual experience has a compassionate voice in two autobiographies by the gay novelist Paul Monette: *Borrowed Time: An AIDS Memoir* (1988) and *Becoming a Man: Half a Life Story* (1992).

Autobiographies number significantly among the masterworks of world culture, particularly in American literature and French literature, and through them the genre has contributed to the formation of cultural values, traditions, and canons. The history of autobiography also offers a record of the cultural and social processes of alteration, redirection, and redefinition. Through autobiography, marginalized individuals, and the social groups to which these individuals belong, have advanced beyond boundaries of silence and victimization to an assertion of the integrity of their own cultural identity and experience.

Notes

CHAPTER 1

1. In James Olney, ed., *Autobiography: Essays Theoretical and Critical* (Princeton, N.J.: Princeton University Press, 1980) two essays by Olney examine the root meanings of *autobiography*: "Autobiography and the Cultural Moment: A Thematic, Historical, and Bibliographical Introduction," 3–27, and "Some Versions of Memory / Some Versions of *Bios*: The Ontology of Autobiography," 236–67.

2. This historical explanation for the emergence of autobiography was first made by James M. Cox, "Autobiography and America," in *Aspects of Narrative*, ed. J. Hillis Miller (New York: Columbia University Press, 1971), 143–72; hereafter cited in text.

3. Georg Misch, *A History of Autobiography in Antiquity*, trans. E. W. Dickes, 2 vols. (1950; reprint, Westport, Conn.: Greenwood Press, 1973); for Misch's commentary on Seneca and Marcus Aurelius, see 2: 417–35, 443–85.

4. Michel de Montaigne, *Essays*, trans. Donald M. Frame (Stanford, Calif.: Stanford University Press, 1958), 611; hereafter cited in text as *Essays*.

5. Benvenuto Cellini, *The Autobiography*, trans. George Bull (New York: Penguin, 1956), 15.

6. Henry David Thoreau, *Walden,* ed. Owen Thomas (New York: Norton, 1966), 1; hereafter cited in text as *Walden.*

7. Jean-Jacques Rousseau, *The Confessions,* trans. J. M. Cohen (New York: Penguin, 1954), 17; hereafter cited in text as *Confessions.*

8. Benjamin Franklin, *Autobiography,* ed. J. A. Leo Lemay and P. M. Zall (New York: Norton, 1986), 1; hereafter cited in text as Franklin.

9. See Marcel Mauss, *Sociology and Psychology,* trans. Ben Brewster (Boston: Routledge and Kegan Paul, 1979).

10. Walt Whitman, *Leaves of Grass,* in *Complete Poetry and Selected Prose,* ed. James E. Miller, Jr. (Boston: Houghton Mifflin, 1959), 27; hereafter cited in text as *Leaves.*

11. Maxim Gorky, *The Autobiography,* trans. Isidor Schneider (Secaucus, N.J.: Citadel Press, 1949), 175.

12. Northrop Frye, *Anatomy of Criticism* (1957; reprint, New York: Atheneum, 1969), 307; hereafter cited in text.

13. Henry Miller, *Tropic of Cancer* (New York: Grove, 1961), 1–2.

14. Jean Thibaudeau, "The Novel as Autobiography," trans. James Goodwin, *Denver Quarterly* 13, no. 3 (Fall 1978): 121–29.

15. Philippe Lejeune, *On Autobiography,* trans. Katherine Leary (Minneapolis: University of Minnesota Press, 1989), "The Autobiographical Pact," 3–30; hereafter cited in text.

16. Emile Benveniste, *Problems in General Linguistics,* trans. Mary Elizabeth Meek (Coral Gables, Fla.: University of Miami Press, 1971), 226. See also Gérard Genette, *Figures of Literary Discourse,* trans. Alan Sheridan (New York: Columbia University Press, 1982), 67–68, 137–43.

CHAPTER 2

1. James M. Cox was the first to explain this interrelation; Cox, 149–55. The relationship between Franklin's career and representational government is further clarified in Michael Warner, "Franklin and the Letters of the Republic," *Representations,* no. 16 (Fall 1986): 110–30.

2. Frye, 83, 140, 243.

3. A strong argument that Part 1 stands as a separate text from the autobiography is made in William H. Shurr, "'Now

Gods, Stand Up for Bastards': Reinterpreting Benjamin Franklin's *Autobiography*," *American Literature* 64, no. 3 (September 1992): 435–51.

4. Franklin is examined in the success story context in Martha Banta, *Failure and Success in America* (Princeton, N.J.: Princeton University Press, 1978), 266–71, 287–92, 294–97; and John G. Cawelti, *Apostles of the Self-Made Man* (Chicago: University of Chicago Press, 1965), 9–23.

5. Benjamin Franklin, *Writings*, ed. J. A. Leo Lemay (New York: Library of America, 1987), 1101; hereafter cited in text as *Writings*.

6. Leo Braudy, *The Frenzy of Renown: Fame and Its History* (New York: Oxford University Press, 1986), 454.

7. Herman Melville, *Israel Potter: His Fifty Years of Exile* (1855; reprint, Garden City, N.Y.: Doubleday, 1965), 61.

8. Max Weber, *The Protestant Ethic and the Spirit of Capitalism*, trans. Talcott Parsons (1920; reprint, New York: Scribners, 1958), 52–54; hereafter cited as Weber. A useful discussion of Franklin in the context of Weber's cultural thesis is Karl J. Weintraub, "The Puritan Ethic and Benjamin Franklin," *Journal of Religion* 56, no. 3 (July 1976): 223–37.

9. Robert F. Sayre, *The Examined Self: Benjamin Franklin, Henry Adams, Henry James* (Princeton, N.J.: Princeton University Press, 1964), 23.

10. Even while he quotes the same passage from the *Autobiography*, the normally thorough Max Weber makes no note of this telling transposition of terms; Weber, 53–54.

11. "The Art of Money Getting" is reprinted in P. T. Barnum, *Struggles and Triumphs* (1869; reprint, New York: Arno Press, 1970), 457–500.

12. Ralph Waldo Emerson, "Wealth," first published in *The Conduct of Life* (1860), in *The Complete Works of Ralph Waldo Emerson*, 12 vols., ed. Edward Waldo Emerson (Boston: Houghton Mifflin: 1903–1906) 6: 125.

13. P. T. Barnum, *The Life of P. T. Barnum, Written by Himself* (New York: Redfield, 1855); *Struggles and Triumphs* (1969; reprint, New York: Arno Press, 1970); *Struggles and Triumphs. . . . Brought Up to 1889* (Buffalo, N.Y.: Courier, 1889).

14. From *A Small Boy and Others* (1913), in Henry James, *Autobiography*, ed. Frederick W. Dupee (London: Allen, 1956), 59.

15. Andrew Carnegie, *The Autobiography of Andrew Carnegie* (Boston: Houghton Mifflin, 1920), 57; hereafter cited in text as *Carnegie.*

16. Lee Iacocca with William Novak, *Iacocca: An Autobiography* (New York: Bantam, 1984), 9; hereafter cited in text as *Iacocca.*

CHAPTER 3

1. Robert B. Stepto, *From Behind the Veil: A Study of Afro-American Narrative* (Urbana, Ill.: University of Illinois Press, 1979), ix. A discussion of Douglass's *Narrative* is contained in Stepto's first chapter, 3–31.

2. Henry Louis Gates, Jr., *Figures in Black: Words, Signs, and the "Racial" Self* (New York: Oxford University Press, 1987), 105. Gates's examination of the issue of literacy in slave narratives is contained on 11–28; his discussion of Frederick Douglass appears on 80–124. Gates continues the examination of this context in *The Signifying Monkey: A Theory of Afro-American Literary Criticism* (New York: Oxford University Press, 1988), 127–69. Valerie Smith engages the issue in *Self-Discovery and Authority in Afro-American Narrative* (Cambridge, Mass.: Harvard University Press, 1987), which includes analysis of Douglass on 20–29. A related discussion of Douglass is provided in Houston A. Baker, Jr., *Blues, Ideology, and Afro-American Literature: A Vernacular Theory* (Chicago: University of Chicago Press, 1984), 39–50.

3. E. D. Hirsch, Jr., *Cultural Literacy: What Every American Needs to Know* (Boston: Houghton Mifflin, 1987), 15.

4. E. D. Hirsch, Jr., Joseph F. Kett, and James Trefil, *The Dictionary of Cultural Literacy* (Boston: Houghton Mifflin, 1988).

5. Paulo Freire and Donaldo Macedo, *Literacy: Reading the Word and the World* (South Hadley, Mass.: Bergin and Garvey Publishers, 1987), 35. Among Freire's other major statements of this position are *Cultural Action for Freedom* (Cambridge, Mass.: Harvard Educational Review, 1970); *Pedagogy of the Oppressed,* trans. Myra Bergman Ramos (New York: Continuum, 1970); and *Education for Critical Consciousness* (New York: Continuum, 1973). Ivan Illich

states related positions in *Deschooling Society* (New York: Harper and Row, 1972) and *Toward a History of Needs* (New York: Pantheon, 1978).

6. Comparisons among the autobiographies are a topic in Eric J. Sundquist, ed., *Frederick Douglass: New Literary and Historical Essays* (New York: Cambridge University Press, 1990), particularly in Sundquist's introduction, 1–22; Wilson J. Moses, "Writing Freely? Frederick Douglass and the Constraints of Racialized Writing," 66–83; David Van Leer, "Reading Slavery: The Anxiety of Ethnicity in Douglass's *Narrative*," 118–40; and Jenny Franchot, "The Punishment of Esther: Frederick Douglass and the Construction of the Feminine," 141–65.

7. Frederick Douglass, *Narrative of the Life of Frederick Douglass, an American Slave, Written by Himself* (New York: Signet, 1968), 119; hereafter cited in text as *Narrative*.

8. Frederick Douglass, *My Bondage and My Freedom* (New York: Dover, 1969), 361–62; hereafter cited in text as *My Bondage*.

9. Frederick Douglass, *Life and Times of Frederick Douglass* (New York: Collier, 1962), 29.

10. William S. McFeely, *Frederick Douglass* (New York: Norton, 1991), 5. McFeely documents Douglass's birth in 1818, while Douglass, later in his life, had calculated it to be 1817. Where the *Narrative* gives specific dates, I have preserved Douglass's estimate of the year.

11. Malcolm X, *The Autobiography of Malcolm X*, reported by Alex Haley (New York: Grove, 1966), 149; hereafter cited in text as *Malcolm*.

12. This description of *The Columbian Orator* is taken from McFeely, 34–36.

13. Direct analogies of Douglass to Franklin are pursued in Rafia Zafar, "Franklinian Douglass: The Afro-American as Representative Man," in Sundquist, 99–117.

14. See 1 Thessalonians 5:2, 4; 2 Peter 3:10; and Revelation 3:3. I am indebted to Van Leer, "Reading Slavery," for these references.

15. *The Frederick Douglass Papers*, 4 vols. to date, ed. John W. Blassingame (New Haven, Conn: Yale University Press, 1979–), vol. 2, 368; hereafter cited in text as *Papers*. An extract from this speech is included in *My Bondage*, 441–45.

16. Harriet Jacobs, *Incidents in the Life of a Slave Girl* (Detroit, Mich.: Negro History Press, 1969), 16; hereafter cited in text as *Incidents.*

17. Richard Wright, *Black Boy: A Record of Childhood and Youth* (New York: Harper and Row, 1966), 48; hereafter cited in text as *Black Boy.*

18. Richard Wright, *American Hunger* (New York: Harper and Row, 1977); hereafter cited in text as *Hunger.* Wright had intended to publish one volume of autobiography in 1945 that contained both the present *Black Boy* and *American Hunger;* his publisher and his editor persuaded him to divide the narrative. *American Hunger* did not receive its first complete publication until 1977.

CHAPTER 4

1. Alice B. Toklas, *What Is Remembered* (New York: Holt, Rinehart and Winston, 1963), 173.

2. *The Selected Writings of Gertrude Stein,* ed. Carl Van Vechten (New York: Vintage, 1962), 237. The *Selected Writings* contains *The Autobiography of Alice B. Toklas* and other important pieces of her writing; hereafter cited in text as *Stein.*

3. Issues of genre in relation to Stein's autobiographies receive attention in Lejeune (46–47 and 250 n. 31) and in James E. Breslin, "Gertrude Stein and the Problem of Autobiography," *Georgia Review* 33, no. 4 (Winter 1979): 901–13. Michael J. Hoffman, ed., *Critical Essays on Gertrude Stein* (Boston: G. K. Hall, 1986) reprints the Breslin essay and includes other important criticism.

4. Two valuable biographical works are Richard Bridgman, *Gertrude Stein in Pieces* (New York: Oxford University Press, 1970); and James R. Mellow, *Charmed Circle: Gertrude Stein and Company* (New York: Avon, 1974).

5. Gertrude Stein, *Narration: Four Lectures* (Chicago: University of Chicago Press, 1935), 14; hereafter cited in text as *Narration.*

6. These stylistic qualities are discussed in detail in Allegra Stewart, *Gertrude Stein and the Present* (Cambridge, Mass.: Harvard University Press, 1967); and Tony Tanner, *The*

Reign of Wonder: Naivety and Reality in American Literature (Cambridge, England: Cambridge University Press, 1965), 187–204.

7. *Selections from Ralph Waldo Emerson,* ed. Stephen E. Whicher (Boston: Houghton Mifflin, 1957), 157.

8. Gertrude Stein, *Lectures in America* (New York: Random, 1935), 231.

9. Gertrude Stein, *Everybody's Autobiography* (New York: Vintage, 1973), 297; hereafter cited in text as *Everybody's Autobiography.*

CHAPTER 5

1. *Essays,* 2; all subsequent references to Montaigne's work will include the book and essay numbers, which are standard, followed by the page number in Donald Frame's English-language edition. I have checked the Frame translation for word choice and style against the French edition *Essais,* 2 vols. (Paris: Garnier, 1962). I provide an alternative to Frame's translation in one instance, which is cited below from the French edition.

2. This passage from the *Essays* is the basis for a brilliant interpretation of Montaigne in Erich Auerbach, *Mimesis: The Representation of Reality in Western Literature,* trans. Willard R. Trask (Princeton, N.J.: Princeton University Press, 1953), 285–311. Two essays valuable to an understanding of the author are Barry Lydgate, "Mortgaging One's Work to the World: Publication and the Structure of Montaigne's *Essais,*" *PMLA* 96, no. 2 (March 1981): 210–23; and Margaret McGowan, "Montaigne: The Self Discovered—*au rebours,*" in *Moy qui me voy: The Writer and the Self from Montaigne to Leiris,* ed. George Craig and McGowan (New York: Oxford University Press, 1989), 1–18. There is also extensive commentary on Montaigne in Michel Beaujour, *Poetics of the Literary Self-Portrait,* trans. Yara Milos (New York: New York University Press, 1991).

3. Montaigne, *Essais,* 3.2, 2:222.

4. I have checked the Cohen translation for word choice and style against the French edition *Les Confessions* (Paris: Garnier, 1964).

5. Further discussion on matters of language and self in the *Confessions* is contained in my essay "Narcissus and Autobiography," *Genre* 12, no. 1 (Spring 1979): 69–92. Valuable treatment of the topic appears in Ernst Cassirer, *The Question of Jean-Jacques Rousseau* (1932), ed. and trans. Peter Gay (Bloomington: Indiana University Press, 1963); Paul de Man, "The Purloined Ribbon," *Glyph* 1 (1977): 28–49; and Huntington Williams, *Rousseau and Romantic Autobiography* (Oxford: Oxford University Press, 1983).

6. I have translated this passage from Rousseau, *Oeuvres complètes*, 3 vols., ed. Bernard Gagnebin and Marcel Raymond (Paris: Gallimard, 1959), vol. 1, 1153–54. Rousseau's inventions in style are evaluated in Jean Starobinski, "The Style of Autobiography," in *Literary Style: A Symposium*, ed. Seymour Chatman (New York: Oxford University Press, 1971): 285–94.

7. Jean-Jacques Rousseau, *Essay on the Origin of Languages*, trans. John H. Moran (New York: Ungar, 1966), 12; hereafter cited in text as *Languages*. Rousseau's *Essay* is a point of departure for extensive speculations on language and representation in Jacques Derrida, *Of Grammatology*, trans. Gayatri Chakravorty-Spivak (Baltimore: Johns Hopkins University Press, 1976).

8. I have altered Cohen's translation in order to suggest more closely the original French in *Les Confessions*, 741.

9. John-Paul Sartre, *The Words*, trans. Bernard Frechtman (New York: Fawcett, 1964), 26; hereafter cited in text as *Words*. I have checked this translation for word choice and style against the French edition *Les Mots* (Paris: Gallimard, 1964).

10. See Jean-Paul Sartre, *Being and Nothingness*, trans. Hazel E. Barnes (New York: Washington Square Press, 1966), 712–34.

11. Jean-Paul Sartre, *Search for a Method*, trans. Hazel E. Barnes (New York: Vintage, 1963), 96.

12. I have altered the translation in order to suggest more closely the original French in *Les Mots*, 117.

13. Jean-Paul Sartre, *The Family Idiot: Gustave Flaubert, 1821–1857* (1971), trans. Carol Cosman, 4 vols. (Chicago: University of Chicago Press, 1981–1991), vol. 1, ix.

14. Jean-Paul Sartre, *What Is Literature?*, trans. Bernard Frechtman (New York: Harper and Row, 1949), 228–29.

15. Jean-Paul Sartre, *The Psychology of Imagination* [trans. not credited] (New York: Citadel, 1948), 263, 265.
16. Roland Barthes, *Roland Barthes by Roland Barthes,* trans. Richard Howard (New York: Hill and Wang, 1977), 142; hereafter cited in text as *Barthes.*
17. Jacques Derrida, *The Post Card: From Socrates to Freud and Beyond,* trans. Alan Bass (Chicago: University of Chicago Press, 1987), 5.

<h3 style="text-align:center">CHAPTER 6</h3>

1. Jean Genet, *The Thief's Journal,* trans. Bernard Frechtman (New York: Grove, 1964), 44–45; hereafter cited in text as *Journal.* I have checked this translation for word choice and style against the French edition *Le Journal du voleur* (Paris: Gallimard, 1949).
2. The place of dialectics in Genet's imagination and their importance in the thought of Hegel leads Jacques Derrida to bring together texts by the two writers and to make wide-ranging, unorthodox philosophical speculations over them in *Glas* (1974), trans. John P. Leavey, Jr., and Richard Rand (Lincoln: University of Nebraska Press, 1986).
3. Genet explores this period of life further in *L'Enfant criminel* (Paris: Paul Morihien, 1949).
4. Sartre makes this act of self-conception the focus of expansive commentary in *Saint Genet: Actor and Martyr* (1952), trans. Bernard Frechtman (New York: New American Library, 1971).
5. Violette Leduc, *La Bâtarde,* trans. Derek Coltman (New York: Farrar, Straus and Giroux, 1965), 3; hereafter cited in text as *Bâtarde.* I have checked this translation for word choice and style against the French edition *La Bâtarde* (Paris: Gallimard, 1964). Isabelle de Courtivron, *Violette Leduc* (Boston: Twayne, 1985) is a valuable, comprehensive critical study of the author.
6. I have modified the translation in order to convey more closely the original French in *La Bâtarde,* 32.
7. Violette Leduc, *In the Prison of Her Skin* (a translation of *L'Asphyxie,* 1946), trans. Derek Coltman (London: Hart-Davis, 1970), 5.

8. Violette Leduc, *Mad in Pursuit,* trans. Derek Coltman (New York: Farrar, Straus and Giroux, 1971), 29.

Bibliographic Essay

The following survey is structured to reflect critical and theoretical concerns pursued in the present study. Cited first are primary bibliographic sources on autobiography and on criticism of the genre, which provide a comprehensive account of publication and scholarship up to 1980. The books and articles before 1980 that are most important in the development of criticism on autobiography are included here. My own survey of criticism concentrates on publications in book form that have appeared since that date. This essay is divided into eleven areas:

1. Bibliography on autobiography and on criticism of the genre
2. Cultural, literary, and psychological definitions of the self
3. Criticism on definitions and issues of autobiography as a genre
4. The uses of autobiography in education, the human sciences, and medicine
5. Spiritual autobiography
6. Women's autobiography, and issues of gender in the genre
7. British autobiography
8. French autobiography
9. American autobiography
10. Ethnic American autobiography
11. Contemporary theory on subjectivity, language, and culture and the study of autobiography

Bibliography on Autobiography and on Criticism of the Genre

William Matthews, *British Autobiographies: An Annotated Bibliography of British Autobiographies Published or Written before 1951* (Berkeley: University of California Press, 1955) provides a brief summary for each entry and indexes its contents by general topic, geographic location, and profession. John Burnett, David Vincent, and David Mayall, eds., *The Autobiography of the Working Class: An Annotated Critical Bibliography*, 3 vols. (Brighton, Sussex: Harvester, 1984–1989) covers publications from 1790 to the present. Each entry includes information on the author's family history, occupation, and activities and on the autobiography's style and content. The indexes list material by topic, location, occupation, and education.

Louis Kaplan, *A Bibliography of American Autobiographies* (Madison: University of Wisconsin Press, 1961) covers publications up to 1945 and includes a subject index that classifies books according to occupation, historical context, and geographic location. Richard G. Lillard, *American Life in Autobiography* (Stanford, Calif.: Stanford University Press, 1956) lists autobiographies in print from 1900 to 1956, arranged by the authors' occupations, and contains a general index. Its main entries include a substantial summary of each autobiography. Mary Louise Briscoe, *American Autobiography, 1945–1980: A Bibliography* (Madison: University of Wisconsin Press, 1982) provides a brief summary with each entry. Its subject index includes headings for historical context, occupation, ethnic and religious backgrounds, and shared kinds of human experience.

Gwenn Davis and Beverly A. Joyce, *Personal Writings by Women to 1900: A Bibliography of American and British Writers* (Norman: University of Oklahoma Press, 1989) covers autobiographies, letters, diaries, and travel literature. The entries represent a complete range of female experience, from accounts by missionaries and pioneer women to those by famous artists and public figures. Where a book's title is insufficiently descriptive, the editors have provided key words to indicate its subject matter. The index gives references by five general topics: type of publication, type of experience, occupation, geographic location, and personal beliefs. Cheryl Cline, *Women's Diaries, Journals, and Letters: An Annotated Bibliography* (New York: Garland, 1989) provides a brief summary of contents for each entry and is indexed by profession, location, subject matter, significant characteristics, and title.

Russell C. Brignano, *Black Americans in Autobiography: An Annotated Bibliography of Autobiographies and Autobiographical Books Written since the Civil War*, rev. and enl. ed. (Durham, N.C.: Duke University Press, 1984) descriptively annotates the contents of each autobiography included. The bibliography contains a section on "Autobiographical Books" that presents other kinds of writing—such as diaries and travel narratives—that address some phase of the author's life. An appendix lists reprints made since 1945 of African-American autobiographies and autobiographical books published before 1865. The book's indexes cover occupations, experiences, organizations, institutions, locations, and year of publication.

H. David Brumble III describes in *An Annotated Bibliography of American Indian and Eskimo Autobiographies* (Lincoln: University of Nebraska Press, 1981) the contents of each narrative and documents the circumstances of its composition. An appendix to his critical study *American Indian Autobiography* (Berkeley: University of California Press, 1988) supplements the earlier bibliography. A similarly annotated bibliography is contained in Gretchen Bataille and Kathleen Sands, *American Indian Women: Telling their Lives* (Lincoln: University of Nebraska Press, 1984).

William Matthews, *Canadian Diaries and Autobiographies* (Berkeley: University of California Press, 1950) provides a brief annotation of contents for most entries and indexes material by major subject areas. Richard Donovon Woods, *Mexican Autobiography: An Annotated Bibliography*, trans. Josefina Cruz-Melendez (New York: Greenwood Press, 1988) offers a full description of the contents of each autobiography. It indexes material by author, title, subject, profession, prominent characteristics, genre, and historical context.

In regard to criticism on autobiography, two comprehensive essays provide valuable guides to scholarship up to 1980. William C. Spengemann, *The Forms of Autobiography: Episodes in the History of a Literary Genre* (New Haven: Yale University Press, 1980) concludes with a 75-page bibliographic essay that documents and reviews the available criticism on the genre. James Olney, ed., *Autobiography: Essays Theoretical and Critical* (Princeton: Princeton University Press, 1980) opens with an essay by Olney, "Autobiography and the Cultural Moment: A Thematic, Historical, and Bibliographical Introduction." In addition to reviewing the field, the essay considers reasons for the long-neglected status of the genre within traditional literary criticism. Paul John Eakin, ed., *American Autobiography: Retrospect and Prospect* (Madison: University of Wisconsin Press, 1991) contains in the editor's Introduction and the contributors' essays very useful accounts of scholarship up to 1990 in the areas of classic American autobiography and ethnic American autobiography.

The *MLA Bibliography*—an annual, comprehensive bibliography of literary scholarship published by the Modern Language Association—has featured an "Autobiography" heading in its subject index since 1981. The journal *Biography* provides a "Current Bibliography on Life-Writing" annually in the Fall issue since it began publication with Volume 1 (1978). New scholarship on autobiography is reviewed regularly in *Biography* and in *a/b: Auto/Biography Studies*. Philippe Lejeune, *Bibliographie des études en langue française sur la littérature personnelle et les récits de vie*, 4 vols. (Nanterre, France: Centre de sémiotique textuelle, 1984–1990) is a comprehensive source for publications in French on the genre. It covers criticism for the period 1982–1989 and indexes the material by names, themes, and era. New autobiographies and other forms of personal writing are listed in its appendix.

DEFINITIONS OF THE SELF

While Sigmund Freud explored the instinct of self-preservation, self is not a category central to his development of psychoanalysis. In the fields of ego psychology and social psychology, however, there are numerous works on the self. Among the books of widest influence are Bruno Bettelheim, *Where the Self Begins* (New York: Macmillan, 1967); Erik H. Erikson, *Childhood and Society* (New York: Norton, 1963) and *Life History and the Historical Moment* (New York: Norton, 1975); Erving Goffmann, *The Presentation of Self in Everyday Life* (New York: Doubleday, 1959); Karen Horney, *Neurosis and Human Growth: The Struggle toward Self-Realization* (New York: Norton, 1950) and *Self-Analysis* (New York:

Norton, 1942); and Harry Stack Sullivan, *The Interpersonal Theory of Psychiatry* (New York: Norton, 1953), which develops concepts of "the self-system." In *Changing the Subject: Psychology, Social Regulation, and Subjectivity* (New York: Methuen, 1984) Julian Henriques, Wendy Hollway, Cathy Urwin, Couze Venn, and Valerie Walkerdine mount a critique of traditional concepts of self and ego in psychology and the social sciences. To displace them, the authors advance a theory of transformational subjectivity.

In the human sciences, Marcel Mauss's *Sociology and Psychology* (1950), trans. Ben Brewster (Boston: Routledge and Kegan Paul, 1979) is an early study in the self as a "category of the human spirit." Exploration through philosophy, religion, psychology, and social history into the self has been extended significantly in the work of Georges Gusdorf, *Les Écritures du moi* (Paris: Jacob, 1991) and *Auto-Bio-Graphie* (Paris: Jacob, 1991). Georg Misch, *A History of Autobiography in Antiquity*, 2 vols., trans. E. W. Dickes (1950; rpt. Westport, Conn.: Greenwood Press, 1973) provides a masterful survey of the origins of individuality and its expression in classical literature.

Anthony Paul Kerby, *Narrative and the Self* (Bloomington: Indiana University Press, 1991) undertakes a broad theoretical study of the relation between language and person. Its guiding thesis is that self is given substance and form primarily through the narrative process. The ground for Kerby's study of this relation is language theory and philosophy rather than literary history. Stephen Greenblatt, *Renaissance Self-Fashioning: From More to Shakespeare* (Chicago: University of Chicago Press, 1980) examines the increased self-consciousness in sixteenth-century England about the fashioning of human identity. Greenblatt pursues the issue through poetry, drama, and prose argument rather than autobiography. Karl Joachim Weintraub, *The Value of the Individual: Self and Circumstance in Autobiography* (Chicago: University of Chicago Press, 1978) follows the thesis that individuality is a distinctly modern mode of conceiving the self. He finds a relative absence of individuality, even in Augustine's *Confessions*, until the Renaissance. From a discussion of Montaigne, Cellini, and the scientist Jerome Cardano, Weintraub continues his study of modern individuation with Gibbon and Rousseau, and he concludes with Goethe, who stands as the creator of an ideal relationship between individuality and the worlds of nature and science.

Another cultural study of individuality places the threshold into modern concepts in a later century: John O. Lyons, *The Invention of the Self: The Hinge of Consciousness in the Eighteenth Century* (Carbondale: Southern Illinois University Press, 1978). From this perspective, during the medieval and Renaissance periods the literary modes of biography generalize the subject, while in the modern period they individualize it. Michel Beaujour, in *Poetics of the Literary Self-Portrait*, trans. Yara Milos (New York: New York University Press, 1991), treats writings representative of the self that do not provide a continuous narrative. Forms such as the meditation, essay, excursus, and speculation comprise, according to Beaujour, a genre distinct from autobiography. In literary self-portraiture, thematic and rhetorical structure takes precedence over chronology and narrative.

Jerome Hamilton Buckley, *The Turning Key: Autobiography and the Subjective Impulse since 1800* (Cambridge: Harvard University Press, 1984) examines a broad range of British poetry and prose for the inwardness of self that defines autobiography. Robert Elbaz, *The Changing Nature of the Self: A Critical Study of the Autobiographic Discourse* (Iowa City: University of Iowa Press, 1987) details an evolving cultural struggle between determinism and freedom in representations of the self from Augustine through Rousseau. Autobiographical discourse displaces and transcends a priori explanations of experience and history through its innovations in subjectivity. A fully modern dynamics of self is examined in the concluding chapter of André Malraux's *Anti-Memoirs*.

Two collections of criticism and commentary treat issues of the self from non-Western perspectives: Martin Kramer, ed., *Middle Eastern Lives: The Practice of Biography and Self-Narrative* (Syracuse, N.Y.: Syracuse University Press, 1991); and Robert E. Hegel and Richard C. Hessney, eds., *Expressions of Self in Chinese Literature* (New York: Columbia University Press, 1985). Matters of self and autobiography in Chinese literature are explored further in Pei-yi Wu, *The Confucian's Progress: Autobiographical Writings in Traditional China* (Princeton: Princeton University Press, 1990).

CRITICISM ON AUTOBIOGRAPHY AS A GENRE

The first important critical books published in English on the genre are Wayne Shumaker, *English Autobiography: Its Emergence, Materials, and Form* (Berkeley: University of California Press, 1954); and Roy Pascal, *Design and Truth in Autobiography* (London: Routledge and Kegan Paul, 1960). Shumaker defines autobiography as a literary mode that gives form to historical experience. While there are problems specific to the literature of fact, autobiography shares similar problems of form with the other representative arts. Pascal proposes that autobiography represents the processes by which the author integrates reality and realizes personal identity. He concludes that the genre is ultimately a form of practical wisdom rather than art.

Over the fifteen years that followed these two groundbreaking books, the thesis that autobiography is indeed an art form is advanced in essays by James M. Cox, Francis R. Hart, William L. Howarth, Alfred Kazin, Barrett J. Mandel, and Jean Starobinski. Some of these essays are gathered in the James Olney collection *Autobiography: Essays Theoretical and Critical* (Princeton: Princeton University Press, 1980). In Olney's book *Metaphors of Self: The Meaning of Autobiography* (Princeton: Princeton University Press, 1972), the genre is considered as a creative act by means of which the metaphors that guide personal narrative also give form to the writer's self.

The scholar who has explored issues of the literary genre most systematically is Philippe Lejeune, in *Le Pacte autobiographique* (Paris: Seuil, 1975), *Je est un autre: l'autobiographie de la littérature aux medias* (Paris: Seuil, 1980), and *Moi aussi* (Paris: Seuil, 1986). Lejeune's concerns range from literary history and cultural issues of literacy to textual properties of person and subjectivity. Selected chapters from these three books have been translated and collected in Philippe Lejeune, *On Autobiography*, trans. Katherine Leary (Minneapolis: University of Minnesota Press, 1989). In *Autobiographical Acts: The Changing Situation of a Literary Genre* (Baltimore: Johns Hopkins University Press, 1976), Elizabeth W. Bruss adopts concepts from a linguistics of the pragmatic and performative functions of language in order to account for the genre as a speech act. Her approach removes the study of autobiography from static categories of literary form and places it instead into the dynamic functions of communication, which are subject to great variation and infinite recombination.

William C. Spengemann takes an approach to the genre grounded in literary history in *The Forms of Autobiography: Episodes in the History of a Literary Genre* (New Haven: Yale University Press, 1980). His book traces the evolution of autobiographical forms from Augustine, Dante, and Bunyan through Franklin, Rousseau, Wordsworth, and Thomas De Quincey. In a last chapter, Spengemann extends the arc of literary evolution to "poetic autobiography," found in nineteenth-century works of prose argument (by Thomas Carlyle) and fiction (by Charles Dickens and Nathaniel Hawthorne). Heidi I. Stull, *The Evolution of the Autobiography from 1770–1850: A Comparative Study and Analysis* (New York: Peter Lang, 1985) concentrates on a segment of literary history in order to emphasize the fundamental changes in the genre made through the autobiographies of Rousseau, Wordsworth, De Quincey, Goethe, and Franz Grillparzer.

Richard N. Coe, *When the Grass Was Taller: Autobiography and the Experience of Childhood* (New Haven: Yale University Press, 1984) maintains that a distinct branch has emerged from the genre. Rousseau and Wordsworth guided Western culture to the modern "discovery" of the meaningfulness of this period in life. While childhood and adolescence is a focus among classic autobiographers like Gide, Gorky, and Stendhal, the study's analysis covers many less prominent writers. Reasoning that in dealing with this period of life the writer engages in compromises between fact and fiction, Coe frequently extends his discussion to poetry and fiction.

Susanna Egan, *Patterns of Experience in Autobiography* (Chapel Hill: University of North Carolina Press, 1984) analyzes four prominent subjects in the genre: the lost innocence of childhood, the heroic journey of youth, spiritual conversion, and confession made in later life. Janet Varner Gunn, *Autobiography: Toward a Poetics of Experience* (Philadelphia: University of Pennsylvania Press, 1982) defines the "autobiographical situation" as a transpersonal interpretative act. The act is conducted on two planes: the autobiographer's reading and reinscription of his or her life, and the reader's responses to the text of autobiography. Gunn applies this poetics of reading the genre to Augustine, Wordsworth, Thoreau, Proust, and Black Elk.

John Pilling, *Autobiography and Imagination: Studies in Self-Scrutiny* (Boston: Routledge and Kegan Paul, 1981) approaches the genre as a form of history of the writer's imagination, where design and theme take precedence over fact. The modern standards for such an act of imagination are set by Henry Adams, Henry James, Yeats, Pasternak, Leiris, Sartre, and Nabokov. Paul Jay, *Being in the Text: Self-Representation from Wordsworth to Roland Barthes* (Ithaca, N.Y.: Cornell University Press, 1984) pursues its central concerns from Romantic autobiography to modernist and postmodern texts. The book takes particular interest in changes in the epistemological status of the self and in reflexive forms of writing.

Paul John Eakin, *Fictions in Autobiography: Studies in the Art of Self-Invention* (Princeton: Princeton University Press, 1985) contends that the self articulated in autobiography is in many important respects a fictive construct. Identity and the truth of experience thus can no longer be treated by a critic of the genre as a stable context mirrored in the content of autobiography. In his subsequent book *Touching the World: Reference in Autobiography* (Princeton: Princeton University Press, 1992), Eakin takes up issues of language, referentiality, and the contexts of historical and biographical fact.

The generic traits identified in the present summary receive further attention in two collections of criticism: Philip Dodd, ed., *Modern Selves: Essays on Modern British and American Autobiography* (Totowa, N.J.: Cass, 1986); and James Olney, ed., *Studies in Autobiography* (New York: Oxford University Press, 1988).

AUTOBIOGRAPHY IN EDUCATION, THE SOCIAL SCIENCES, AND MEDICINE

Two college-level anthologies present autobiography as a subject for the instruction of writing and critical thinking: Roger J. Porter and H. R. Wolf, *The Voice Within: Reading and Writing Autobiography* (New York: Knopf, 1973); and Robert Lyons, *Autobiography: A Reader for Writers* (New York: Oxford University Press, 1977). William Zinsser, ed., *Inventing the Truth: The Art and Craft of Memoir* (Boston: Houghton Mifflin, 1987) gathers essays on life-writing by American authors Russell Baker, Annie Dillard, Alfred Kazin, and Toni Morrison.

Pioneer research on the roles of self-representation in the social sciences is reported in Gordon W. Allport, *The Use of Personal Documents in Psychological Science* (New York: Social Science Research Council, 1942); and Louis Gottschalk, Clyde Kluckhohn, and Robert Angell, *The Use of Personal Documents in History, Anthropology, and Sociology* (New York: Social Science Research Council, 1945). For the discipline of anthropology, this investigation is extended in L. L. Langness, *The Life History in Anthropological Science* (New York: Holt, 1965); and L. L. Langness and Gelya Frank, *Lives: An Anthropological Approach to Biography* (Novato, Calif.: Chandler and Sharp, 1981), which contains a 50-page bibliography.

Gelya Frank applies the same anthropological method in *Venus on Wheels: The Life History of a Congenital Amputee* (Doctoral Dissertation, Department of Anthropology, UCLA, 1981). A study that examines the functions of autobiography in the health sciences is James E. Birren and Donna E. Deutchman, *Guiding Autobiography Groups for Older Adults: Exploring the Fabric of Life* (Baltimore: Johns Hopkins University Press, 1991).

SPIRITUAL AUTOBIOGRAPHY

Anne Hunsaker Hawkins, *Archetypes of Conversion: The Autobiographies of Augustine, Bunyan, and Merton* (Cranbury, N.J.: Associated University Presses, 1985) discusses the three major spiritual autobiographers in terms of archetypes (life as a pilgrimage, for example) and generic traits (such as the patterns of sacred meaning that emerge from life's pilgrimage). Heather Henderson, *The Victorian Self: Autobiography and Biblical Narrative* (Ithaca, N.Y.: Cornell University Press, 1989) focuses on three works of spiritual analysis and inquiry: Cardinal Newman's *Apologia Pro Vita Sua*, John Ruskin's *Praeterita*, and Edmund Gosse's *Father and Son*. Starting from the tradition of religious confession, Jeremy Tambling, *Confession: Sexuality, Sin, the Subject* (New York: Manchester University Press, 1990) progresses through other contexts such as the criminal investigation, the clinical examination, and the philosophical inquiry.

Daniel B. Shea, *Spiritual Autobiography in Early America* (first published 1968; Madison: University of Wisconsin Press, 1988) closely examines two principal types: Quaker journals and Puritan spiritual narratives. Virginia Lieson Brereton, *From Sin to Salvation: Stories of Women's Conversions, 1800 to the Present* (Bloomington: Indiana University Press, 1991) concerns Protestant conversion narratives by American women. Joseph Fichtelberg, *The Complex Image: Faith and Method in American Autobiography* (Philadelphia: University of Pennsylvania Press, 1989) grounds its inquiry in the methods of re-vision set forth in Nietzsche's *Ecce Homo*. The critical analysis that follows examines a millennial strain in American autobiography identified with John Woolman, Benjamin Franklin, Frederick Douglass, Walt Whitman, W. E. B. Du Bois, and Gertrude Stein.

WOMEN'S AUTOBIOGRAPHY AND ISSUES OF GENDER

Over the past fifteen years, women's studies have been 'an area of rich scholarly and critical activity, and this activity is strongly represented in the study of autobiography. The collection *Women's Autobiography: Essays in Criticism* (Bloomington: Indiana University Press, 1980), edited by Estelle C. Jelinek, assembles examples of this new scholarship in its early phase. Carolyn G. Heilbrun, *Writing a Woman's Life* (New York: Norton, 1988) presents a concise statement of important issues of gender in the genre. Heilbrun identifies a split between the old genre of women's autobiography, "which tends to find beauty even in pain and to transform rage into spiritual acceptance" (12), and a new genre by women who admit anger and openly identify their desires for power and control in personal experience. The last chapter provides an autobiographical account of why she, as a professor of literature, published detective fictions under the pseudonym Amanda Cross. Mary Catherine Bateson in her book *Composing a Life* (New York: Atlantic Monthly Press, 1989) combines a study of five contemporary women with self-study in order to examine common female experiences of friendship, caretaking, commitment, work, and partnership.

Sidonie Smith, *A Poetics of Women's Autobiography: Marginality and the Fictions of Self-Representation* (Bloomington: Indiana University Press, 1987) develops its subject in the face of normative definitions of the genre that have largely kept women's writings at the margins of critical discussion. Smith's poetics details the distinct traditions, perspectives on experience, and conceptions of self that arise from gender difference. Women writing in the genre are engaged in negotiation with the cultural—and often paternal—imperatives of subjectivity, language, family identity, and social roles.

Leonore Hoffmann and Margo Culley, eds., *Women's Personal Narratives: Essays in Criticism and Pedagogy* (New York: Modern Language Association, 1985) gathers criticism on modes of personal expression such as oral testimony, letters, and the diary and offers suggestions on the uses of such autobiographical forms in the classroom. Shari Benstock, ed., *The Private Self: Theory and Practice of Women's Autobiographical Writings* (Chapel Hill: University of North Carolina Press, 1988) contains essays that draw on contemporary theories of language and subjectivity in their consideration of texts from French, British, and American literature. Theoretical concerns extend to referentiality, textuality, and feminism in Bella Brodzki and Celeste Schenck, eds., *Life / Lines: Theorizing Women's Autobiography* (Ithaca, N.Y.: Cornell University Press, 1988). The forms and contexts of women's self-representation are also extended in this volume, with essays on women film directors, an Egyptian feminist, and the Latin American testimonial.

Much recent research and scholarship has contributed to the making of a literary history of women's autobiography. Many eras in that literary history are surveyed in Estelle C. Jelinek, *The Tradition of Women's Autobiography from Antiquity to the Present* (Boston: Twayne, 1986); and Domna C. Stanton, ed., *The Female Autograph: Theory and Practice of Autobiography from the Tenth to the Twentieth Century* (Chicago: University of Chicago Press, 1987).

Specific areas within the larger literary history are the subject of other books: Elspeth Graham et al., eds., *Her Own Life: Autobiographical Writings by Seventeenth-Century Englishwomen* (New York: Routledge, 1989); Faith Evelyn Beasley, *Revising Memory: Women's Fiction and Memoirs in Seventeenth-Century France* (New Brunswick, N.J.: Rutgers University Press, 1990); Felicity Nussbaum, *The Autobiographical Subject: Gender and Ideology in Eighteenth-Century England* (Baltimore: Johns Hopkins University Press, 1989); Katherine Goodman, *Dis/closures: Women's Auto-*

biography in Germany between 1790 and 1914 (New York: Peter Lang, 1986); Julia Swindells, *Victorian Writing and Working Women: The Other Side of Silence* (Minneapolis: University of Minnesota Press, 1985); and Mary Jean Corbett, *Representing Femininity: Middle-Class Subjectivity in Victorian and Edwardian Women's Autobiographies* (New York: Oxford University Press, 1992).

The compounded cultural issues of gender and race are a matter of increased attention in studies of the genre. Francoise Lionnet, *Autobiographical Voices: Race, Gender, Self-Portraiture* (Ithaca, N.Y.: Cornell University Press, 1989) engages in a comparative analysis of African-American, Caribbean, and Indian Ocean autobiographies by women. Her goal is to identify the elements of plurality and difference in autobiography that make for culturally potent heterogeneity. Discussion of related issues is contained in the essays collected in Susan Groag Bell and Marilyn Yalom, eds., *Revealing Lives: Autobiography, Biography, and Gender* (Albany: State University of New York Press, 1990).

Joanne M. Braxton, *Black Women Writing Autobiography: A Tradition within a Tradition* (Philadelphia: Temple University Press, 1989) starts from a consideration of the tradition's formation in slave narratives and in the narratives of freeborn African-American women of the nineteenth century. Zora Neale Hurston and Maya Angelou provide a focus for the book's discussion of twentieth-century autobiographers. King-Kok Cheung, *Articulate Silences: Double-Voiced Discourse in Hisaye Yamamoto, Maxine Hong Kingston, and Joy Kogawa* (Ithaca, N.Y.: Cornell University Press, 1993) places these three Asian-American writers in the cultural context of a female rhetoric, where strategies of reticence, indirection, and irony are powerful conventions.

The Personal Narratives Group, a collective of scholars based at the University of Minnesota, has gathered its criticism in *Interpreting Women's Lives: Feminist Theory and Personal Narratives* (Bloomington: Indiana University Press, 1989). Particular attention is paid to the interpersonal contexts distinctive in women's autobiography and to the genre's influential roles in the history of liberationist and feminist movements. Nancy K. Miller, *Getting Personal: Feminist Occasions and Other Autobiographical Acts* (New York: Routledge, 1991) opens with an explanation of the importance of self-representation for the politics and culture of feminism. Other chapters examine issues such as feminist pedagogy and autobiography in the classroom. The occasion for these discussions arises from Miller's autobiography as a university professor, which recounts matters such as department politics for the woman faculty member and her exchange of ideas at academic conferences. Miller believes that "personal criticism," a fabric of "self-narrative woven into critical argument" (2), is a basis upon which to extend feminist scholarship.

BRITISH AUTOBIOGRAPHY

The first study to treat autobiography as a distinct genre within British literature is Wayne Shumaker, *English Autobiography: Its Emergence, Materials, and Form*. The book traces the genre's evolution from origins such as travel accounts, memoirs, spiritual narratives, and secular confessions. Paul Delany, *British Autobiography in the Seventeenth Century* (London: Routledge and Kegan Paul, 1969) concentrates on these origins, with equal attention to religious accounts and to personal narratives of secular experience. Patricia Ann Meyer Spacks, *Imagining a Self: Autobiography and Novel in Eighteenth-Century England* (Cambridge: Harvard University Press, 1976) compares the literary artifices required in each genre. Autobiography is studied through the journals and memoirs of James Boswell, William Cowper, Fanny Burney, and Edward Gibbon, the novel through works by Burney, Henry Fielding, Laurence Sterne, and Samuel Richardson. One important distinction Spacks makes between the genres is that while autobiography depends upon a rhetoric of explanation, the novel requires the creation and control of a meaningful plot.

Jonathan Loesberg, *Fictions of Consciousness: Mill, Newman, and the Reading of Victorian Prose* (New Brunswick, N.J.: Rutgers University Press, 1986) analyzes the major Victorian autobiographies by Mill and Newman in the context of the authors' philosophical arguments on matters of history, mind, and will. Linda H. Peterson, *Victorian Autobiography: The Tradition of Self-Interpretation* (New Haven: Yale University Press, 1986) asserts that the process of self-interpretation, derived from principles of biblical interpretation, defines a distinctly English mode within the genre. From this perspective, the religious confession by John Bunyan is a primary antecedent to Victorian autobiography, even in the case of a writer like John Ruskin, who resists the genre's spiritual traditions. Further studies of this period in the genre are collected in George P. Landow, ed., *Approaches to Victorian Autobiography* (Athens: Ohio University Press, 1979).

Avrom Fleishman, *Figures of Autobiography: The Language of Self-Writing in Victorian and Modern England* (Berkeley: University of California Press, 1983) opens with a review of the critical approaches—from stylistic and mythic to structural—that have dominated literary analysis of the genre. Fleishman identifies continuity within the genre in its *figures*: the formative concepts, images, and verbal conventions of its literary discourse. From this foundation, his study examines a number of autobiographers (including Mill, Newman, and Yeats) and autobiographical novelists (such as Dickens, Joyce, and Woolf). Regenia Gagnier, *Subjectivities: A History of Self-Representation in Britain, 1832–1920* (New York: Oxford University Press, 1991) organizes its materials by social class and gender in order to provide analysis of Victorian subjectivity. Gagnier's primary interest lies with the cultural rhetoric that constructs gender and group identity for the working and middle classes and for the intelligentsia.

Carl Dawson, *Prophets of Past Time: Seven British Autobiographers, 1880–1914* (Baltimore: Johns Hopkins University Press, 1988) defines a branch of the genre wherein narrative is based in the interactions of memory and imagination and is combined with the autobiographer's profound reflection on these two faculties. William Hale White, Father George Tyrell, Edmund Gosse, George Moore, Samuel Butler, Ford Maddox Ford, and William Butler Yeats are the autobiographers explored at length in Dawson's study. A. O. J. Cockshut, *The Art of Autobiography in 19th and 20th Century England* (New Haven: Yale University Press, 1984) arranges material by character type and categories of experience, with particular emphasis on the childhood phases of life. Brian Finney, *The Inner I: British Literary Autobiography of the Twentieth Century* (New York: Oxford University Press, 1985) concentrates on the varieties of subjectivity in life accounts by imaginative writers. The book's first section surveys the narrative versions of truth typical of the genre, from the factual inventory to the ironic self-study. A second section investigates the many modes through which identity is posited in autobiography: the contexts of myth, dream, spirituality, and history and the patterns of development manifest in childhood.

FRENCH AUTOBIOGRAPHY

Philippe Lejeune, *L'Autobiographie en France* (Paris: Colin, 1971) surveys its topic in several different ways. Early chapters are directed toward definition of the genre, construction of its history, and the interpretation of texts. Subsequent sections provide a descriptive chronology, an anthology of excerpts that illustrate varieties of "the autobiographical pact," and a collection of theoretical and critical statements on matters related to the genre. George Craig and Margaret McGowan, eds., *Moy qui me voy: The Writer and the Self from Montaigne to Leiris* (New York: Oxford University Press, 1989) contains critical essays on the versions of self in classics of French autobiography (Montaigne, Rousseau, Hugo, Sartre, and Leiris) and on the problematics of self in French thought (Blaise Pascal) and French fiction (Flaubert, Proust, and Camus).

Huntington Williams, *Rousseau and Romantic Autobiography* (Oxford: Oxford University Press, 1983) studies this author as the model for modern autobiography based on his revolutionary cultural act of constructing personal identity essentially through his own writing. Rousseau broke earlier traditions of self-study with his assertion of the Romantic values of sentiment, reverie, love, friendship, and nature. In addition to the *Confessions*, Williams analyzes *Rousseau juge de Jean-Jacques: Dialogues* (written 1772–1776) and *Rêveries d'un promeneur solitaire* (written 1776–1778) as extensions of Rousseau's autobiographical project.

Serge Doubrovsky bases his study *Autobiographiques: de Corneille à Sartre* (Paris: Presses Universitaires de France, 1988) on the premise that through analytic reading the *critic* authors an intimate autobiography of the writer. He starts the process with a reading of the dynamics of sexuality and gender in the plays of the seventeenth-century dramatist Corneille. After a more direct discussion of the autobiography by Michel Leiris, Doubrovsky turns to a psychoanalysis of his own novel *Fils* (Son; 1977). The book's concluding three chapters treat the problems of autobiographical representation in Sartre's novel *Nausea* (1938) and in his published notebooks, letters, and essays. Germaine Brée, *Narcissus Absconditus: The Problematic Art of Autobiography in Contemporary France* (Oxford: Clarendon Press, 1978) reprints her lecture on the textual identities—as distinct from biographical identities—of Leiris, Genet, Sartre, and Barthes in their autobiographies.

AMERICAN AUTOBIOGRAPHY

Robert F. Sayre, in *The Examined Self: Benjamin Franklin, Henry Adams, Henry James* (Princeton, N.J.: Princeton University Press, 1964), a major early critical work in the field, values self-examination by these autobiographers as a process that profoundly reflects American experience. James M. Cox, *Recovering Literature's Lost Ground: Essays in American Autobiography* (Baton Rouge: Louisiana State University Press, 1989) reprints all the essays on the subject by this important critic, starting with his influential piece "Autobiography and America," first published in 1971. The autobiographers Cox treats include Thomas Jefferson, Ulysses S. Grant, Booker T. Washington, Henry Adams, and Henry James. Thomas Cooley, *Educated Lives: The Rise of Modern Autobiography in America* (Columbus: Ohio State University Press, 1976) defines a specific mode in the genre of "education," as opposed to "cultivation." Education designates the self's struggle with external forces, through which an individual gains some fragmentary, unstable knowledge. While self-cultivation is exemplified by Franklin and Thoreau, education is the mode of autobiographies by Adams, Twain, Howells, and James.

Mutlu Konuk Blasing, *The Art of Life: Studies in American Autobiographical Literature* (Austin: University of Texas Press, 1977) treats the genre as unique in the degree to which it reveals the dynamics of creation. This study's primary interest is in the conversion of history into consciousness and of consciousness into literary form, a process examined in the prose of Thoreau, James, and Adams and in the poetry of Whitman, William Carlos Williams, and Frank O'Hara. G. Thomas Couser, *American Autobiography: The Prophetic Mode* (Amherst: University of Massachusetts Press, 1979) defines a distinct mode wherein the autobiographer assumes the role of prophet in creating unity between personal and communal experience. For Couser this mode constitutes a major, continuous tradition from the Puritans to contemporary autobiographical writers like Norman Mailer and Robert Pirsig.

Albert E. Stone, ed., *The American Autobiography: A Collection of Critical Essays* (Englewood Cliffs, N.J.: Prentice-Hall, 1981) gathers criticism representative of approaches to autobiography within American studies up through the 1970s. Stone's own critical study *Autobiographical Occasions and Original Acts: Versions of American Identity from Henry Adams to Nate Shaw* (Philadelphia: University of Pennsylvania Press, 1982) offers a comprehensive survey of modern American autobiography. In the face of critical trends that treat autobiography primarily as a branch of imaginative literature, Stone favors a balanced perspective that also accounts for the historical and ideological dimensions in the genre that represent cultural issues larger than the self. Philip Abbott, *States of Perfect Freedom: Autobiography and American Political Thought* (Amherst: University of Massachusetts Press, 1987) adopts such an approach in treating the genre in relation to American political traditions of consensus. Abbott's book is concerned with a pattern of conversion experience left incomplete and thus productive of a subversive individualism. This thesis leads to an unusual and suggestive grouping of autobiographers, such as that of Abbie Hoffman and Malcolm X with Benjamin Franklin.

Herbert Leibowitz, *Fabricating Lives: Explorations in American Autobiography* (New York: Knopf, 1989) places the genre within an encompassing theme of American culture: the individual's quest for distinction. Exemplary texts—such as the autobiographies of Franklin, Goldman, Jane Addams, Stein, Wright, and the architect Louis Sullivan—debate the power and integrity of such American ideals in the course of narrating that quest. G. Thomas Couser, *Altered Egos: Authority in American Autobiography* (New York: Oxford University Press, 1989) starts from a consideration of the fraudulent *Autobiography of Howard Hughes*. Couser goes on to examine the problematic social and historical status of the autobiographer's "I" in narratives by Franklin, Douglass, Jacobs, Barnum, Twain, Black Elk, and other Americans. Timothy Dow Adams, *Telling Lies in Modern American Autobiography* (Chapel Hill: University of North Carolina Press, 1990) considers the constituents of autobiography—self, life, and writing—and the expectations of design and truth in the genre to be in paradoxical relationship with one another. The key to the clarification of autobiography thus becomes analysis of the genre as an art of lying, which Adams pursues in chapters on Stein, Sherwood Anderson, Wright, Mary McCarthy, and Lillian Hellman.

Gordon O. Taylor, *Chapters of Experience: Studies in 20th Century American Autobiography* (New York: St. Martin's Press, 1983) assesses a modern situation for the genre wherein the documentary and the imaginative motives for writing are inseparable. Starting with Henry Adams, Taylor's study explores this situation in books by Henry James, W. E. B. Du Bois, Malcolm X, James Agee, Mary McCarthy, Edmund Wilson, Michael Herr, and Joan Didion. Two collections reflect other interests in recent criticism on the genre: A. Robert Lee, ed., *First Person Singular: Studies in American Autobiography* (London: Vision, 1988); and J. Bill Berry, ed., *Located Lives: Place and Idea in Southern Autobiography* (Athens: University of Georgia Press, 1990). Paul John Eakin, ed., *American Autobiography: Retrospect and Prospect* (Madison: University of Wisconsin Press, 1991) provides valuable reviews of scholarship and recent critical perspectives on the canon of American autobiography and on prominent works in the genre from ethnic American literatures.

ETHNIC AMERICAN AUTOBIOGRAPHY

An introductory survey of this field useful to both students and teachers is James Craig Holte, *The Ethnic I: A Sourcebook for Ethnic-American Autobiography* (New York: Greenwood Press, 1988). Each entry for the survey's twenty-nine autobiographers features a biographical summary, an account of the autobiography's contents, a brief critical assessment, and a selected bibliography. The first area within the general field to receive broad scholarly attention was the slave narrative. Frances Smith Foster, *Witnessing Slavery: The Development of Ante-Bellum Slave Narratives* (Westport, Conn.: Greenwood Press, 1979) writes a literary history of the genre in that period. Arguing that slave narratives over the three decades prior to the Civil War intensify the depiction of slaveholding violence and of African-American humanity, the study demonstrates the lines of tradition and change in the genre. William L. Andrews, *To Tell a Free Story: The First Century of Afro-American Autobiography, 1760–1865* (Urbana: University of Illinois Press, 1986) provides generic definitions that entail two dynamics: the relationship of the narrator to a white reading audience, and the strategies through which the narrator verifies his or her experience and humanity. Andrews locates a major shift within the genre in the 1840s, when the autobiographer

153

begins to write independently of any internalized voice of white moral authority. As a consequence, the narrator moves toward a social and psychological position of increased marginality.

Further criticism on this category of the genre is available in John Sekora and Darwin T. Turner, eds., *The Art of Slave Narrative: Original Essays in Criticism and Theory* (Macomb: Western Illinois University Press, 1982); and Charles T. Davis and Henry Louis Gates, Jr., eds., *The Slave's Narrative* (New York: Oxford University Press, 1985). The Davis and Gates book collects recent criticism and, most valuably, reviews from newspapers and journals published originally in the period 1750–1861. The critical essays are divided into two perspectives: the slave narrative as a historical source and as literature.

Stephen Butterfield, *Black Autobiography in America* (Amherst: University of Massachusetts Press, 1974) starts with an examination of the slave narrative and moves forward through consideration of books by Richard Wright, James Baldwin, Maya Angelou, Anne Moody, and other modern autobiographers. Sidonie Smith, *Where I'm Bound: Patterns of Slavery and Freedom in Black American Autobiography* (Westport, Conn.: Greenwood Press, 1974) maintains that the thematic and structural features of slave narratives determined prototypes for subsequent African-American autobiographers. The prototypes involve opposed tendencies. One tendency entails a radical break from inhuman social conditions and the suppression of self; the other entails the achievement of a place within society and authentic self-expression.

Other studies with important chapters on African-American autobiography have been cited previously in my discussion of Frederick Douglass: Robert B. Stepto, *From Behind the Veil: A Study of Afro-American Narrative* (Urbana: University of Illinois Press, 1979); Valerie Smith, *Self-Discovery and Authority in Afro-American Narrative* (Cambridge: Harvard University Press, 1987); and Henry Louis Gates, Jr., *Figures in Black: Words, Signs, and the "Racial" Self* (New York: Oxford University Press, 1987). In *My Father's Shadow: Intergenerational Conflict in African American Men's Autobiography* (Philadelphia: University of Pennsylvania Press, 1991), David L. Dudley examines seven autobiographers— Douglass, Washington, Du Bois, Wright, Baldwin, Eldridge Cleaver, and Malcolm X—in the context of masculine myths of individual triumph long dominant in mainstream American culture. The study also charts the anxieties of political and literary influence among these autobiographers.

Joanne M. Braxton, *Black Women Writing Autobiography: A Tradition within a Tradition* (Philadelphia: Temple University Press, 1989), and King-Kok Cheung, *Articulate Silences: Double-Voiced Discourse* (Ithaca, N.Y.: Cornell University Press, 1992) have been described already, in the category of women's studies. Gretchen Bataille and Kathleen Sands, *American Indian Women: Telling Their Lives* (Lincoln: University of Nebraska Press, 1984) applies an analytic system that divides texts within the field into ethnographic autobiography and literary autobiography. Such division is not equivalent to one between oral and written autobiography, for the study categorizes as literary several autobiographies that were reported orally by the subject to a collaborator. From this point of departure, the two scholars discuss in detail texts by Maria Chona, Mountain Wolf Woman, Maria Campbell, and other Native Americans.

Arnold Krupat, *For Those Who Come After: A Study of Native American Autobiography* (Berkeley: University of California Press, 1985) has selected narratives in order to demonstrate their contexts in history, their relationships with the human sciences and with literature, and their correlation to the plot archetypes of romance, tragedy, comedy, and irony. Krupat's critical goal is to establish the origin, types, and functions of Native American autobiography as a specific genre. H. David Brumble, *American Indian Autobiography* (Berkeley: University of California Press, 1988) adopts different criteria by starting from the preliterate traditions within Indian cultures. Brumble also engages the problematic roles editors, collaborators, anthropologists, and ghost writers have played in the creation of Native American texts. The Brumble study brings analysis historically up through the contemporary writer N. Scott Momaday, as does Hertha Dawn Wong, *Sending My Heart Back across the Years: Tradition and Innovation in Native American Autobiography* (New York: Oxford University Press, 1992). Nonwritten forms of personal narrative, tribal contexts, and non-Western concepts of self have created a unique cultural situation for the genre. Wong's historical inquiry into its traditions and development starts with evidence from the pre-Columbian period, before contact with European cultures, in the forms of pictographic paintings and naming practices. From her critical perspective, the traditions of oral cultures remain manifest in the written record of Native American autobiography into the present.

CONTEMPORARY THEORY AND THE STUDY OF AUTOBIOGRAPHY

The critiques of society, language, culture, and individuality conducted over the last four decades in the human sciences have influenced our understanding of the core concepts of self, life, and writing that comprise the genre autobiography. Over this period, the French analyst Jacques Lacan has engaged in a complete rethinking of Freudian psychoanalysis. Lacan's theories elaborate the dependency of subjectivity upon symbolic formation and language, starting with the early paper "The Mirror Stage as Formative of the Function of the I" (1949), in Lacan, *Écrits: A Selection*, trans. Alan Sheridan (New York: Norton, 1977). A comprehensive inquiry into this matter is made in Lacan's *The Language of the Self: The Function of Language in Psychoanalysis* (1956), ed. and trans. Anthony Wilden (Baltimore: Johns Hopkins University Press, 1968). Wilden provides extended commentary that clarifies Lacan's terminology and differentiates his concepts from Freud's.

Application of a revised psychoanalysis to criticism of the genre is pursued by Jeffrey Mehlman's *A Structural Study of Autobiography: Proust, Leiris, Sartre, Lévi-Strauss* (Ithaca, N.Y.: Cornell University Press, 1974). The inclusion of the novelist Proust in Mehlman's study indicates the problematic status of the two genres in modernist writing. Two other critics to treat the novelist's lifework of writing as virtually a form of autobiography are Edward Said, "Notes on the Characterization of a Literary Text," *MLN* 85, no. 6 (December 1970): 765–90, and Jean Thibaudeau, "The Novel as Autobiography," trans. James Goodwin, *Denver Quarterly* 13, no. 3 (Fall 1978): 121–29.

A rethinking of cultural forms has led critics to question the conventional definitions of genre. Jacques Derrida contends that while genre appears to pose a law constituted by limits and norms, the text engages in a counter-law that limitlessly admixes norms: "The Law of Genre," trans. Avital Rowell, *Critical Inquiry* 7, no. 1 (Autumn 1980): 55–81. Paul de Man argues that autobiography is representative of writing, not of life, and that it is structured through "a figure of reading," not through generic conventions: "Autobiography as De-facement," *MLN* 94, no. 5 (December 1979): 919–30.

Derrida investigates subjectivity and textuality in ways that bear directly on autobiography in *The Post Card: From Socrates to Freud and Beyond* (1980), trans. Alan Bass (Chicago: University of Chicago Press, 1987), where Freud's *Beyond the Pleasure Principle* is analyzed as an "auto-biography of *writing*"; in *The Ear of the Other: Otobiography, Transference, Translation* (1982), ed. Christie McDonald, trans. Peggy Kamuf (Lincoln: University of Nebraska Press, 1988), which adopts a similar approach to Nietzsche's *Ecce Homo*; and in "Signature Event Context," in Derrida, *Margins of Philosophy*, trans. Samuel Weber and Jeffrey Mehlman (Chicago: University of Chicago Press, 1982).

Matters of authorial identity and textual authority, which are at the center of any definition of the genre, are contested vigorously in contemporary theory. Prominent in the debate are the positions taken in Michel Foucault, "What Is an Author?" in Foucault, *Language, Counter-Memory, Practice*, ed. Donald F. Bouchard, trans. Donald F. Bouchard and Sherry Simon (Ithaca, N.Y.: Cornell University Press, 1977); and Roland Barthes, "The Death of the Author" and "From Work to Text" in Barthes, *Image-Music-Text*, trans. Stephen Heath (New York: Hill and Wang, 1977). Peggy Kamuf summarizes issues in the debate and makes her own original contribution with *Signature Pieces: On the Institution of Authorship* (Ithaca, N.Y.: Cornell University Press, 1988).

Recommended Autobiographies: A Selected List

The date of first publication in the original language, and other information where pertinent, is given immediately after the book title.

Abélard, Pierre. *Historia Calamitatum* (written 1129). In *The Letters of Abélard and Héloïse*. Trans. Betty Radice. New York: Penguin, 1974.

Acosta, Oscar Zeta. *The Autobiography of a Brown Buffalo* (1972). New York: Popular Library, 1972.

Adams, Henry. *The Education of Henry Adams* (printed privately 1907; published 1918). Ed. Ernest Samuels. Boston: Houghton Mifflin, 1973.

Addams, Jane. *Forty Years at Hull-House* (1935). New York: Macmillan, 1935.

———. *Twenty Years at Hull-House* (1910). Urbana: University of Illinois Press, 1990.

Agee, James. *Let Us Now Praise Famous Men: Three Tenant Families* (1941). With the collaboration of photographer Walker Evans. Boston: Houghton Mifflin, 1980.

Akutagawa, Ryunosuke. *A Fool's Life* (1927). Trans. Will Petersen. Hygiene, Colo.: Eridanos Press, 1987.

Anderson, Sherwood. *Sherwood Anderson's Memoirs* (1942). Chapel Hill: University of North Carolina Press, 1969.

———. *A Story-Teller's Story* (1924). Cleveland, Ohio: Press of Case Western Reserve University, 1968.

————. *Tar: A Midwest Childhood* (1926). Cleveland, Ohio: Press of Case Western Reserve University, 1969.

Angelou, Maya. *I Know Why the Caged Bird Sings* (1970). New York: Bantam, 1971.

Antin, Mary. *The Promised Land* (1912). New York: Houghton Mifflin, 1912.

Anzaldúa, Gloria. *Borderlands/La Frontera: The New Mestiza* (1987). San Francisco, Calif.: Spinsters/Aunt Lute, 1987.

Augustine, Saint. *Confessions* (ca. 400). Trans. John K. Ryan. Garden City, N.Y.: Image Books, 1960.

Baker, Russell. *The Good Times* (1989). New York: Morrow, 1989.

————. *Growing Up* (1982; Pulitzer Prize). New York: New American Library, 1983.

Baldwin, James. *The Fire Next Time* (1963). New York: Dial, 1963.

————. *Nobody Knows My Name* (1961). New York: Dial, 1961.

————. *Notes of a Native Son* (1955). Boston: Beacon, 1955.

Banks, Ann, ed. *First-Person America*. New York: Vintage, 1981.

Barnum, P. T. *The Life of P. T. Barnum, Written by Himself* (1855). New York: Redfield, 1855.

————. *Struggles and Triumphs* (1869). New York: Arno Press, 1970.

————. *Struggles and Triumphs, . . . Brought up to 1889* (1889). Buffalo, N.Y.: Courier, 1889.

Barthes, Roland. *Roland Barthes by Roland Barthes* (1975). Trans. Richard Howard. New York: Hill and Wang, 1977.

Berenson, Bernard. *Sketch for a Self-Portrait* (1949). New York: Pantheon, 1949.

Berkman, Alexander. *Prison Memoirs of an Anarchist* (1912). New York: Schocken, 1970.

Black Elk. *Black Elk Speaks, Being the Life Story of a Holy Man of the Oglala Sioux* (1932). Reported by John G. Neihardt. New York: Pocket Books, 1972.

Brown, Claude. *Manchild in the Promised Land* (1965). New York: New American Library, 1965.

Brown, William Wells. *Narrative of William Wells Brown, A Fugitive Slave* (1847); *The American Fugitive in Europe. Sketches of Places and People Abroad* (1855). Collected in *The Travels of William Wells Brown*. New York: Markus Weiner, 1991.

Bulosan, Carlos. *America Is in the Heart: A Personal History* (1946). Seattle: University of Washington Press, 1973.

Buñuel, Luis. *My Last Sigh* (1982). Trans. Abigail Israel. New York: Knopf, 1983.

Bunyan, John. *Grace Abounding to the Chief of Sinners* (six editions in the years 1666 to 1688, the year of his death). Ed. Roger Sharrock. Oxford: Clarendon Press, 1962.

Burnett, John, ed. *Annals of Labour: Autobiographies of British Working-Class People, 1820–1920*. Bloomington: Indiana University Press, 1974.

Cahan, Abraham. *The Education of Abraham Cahan* (published in 5 vols. 1926–1931). Trans. Leon Stein, Abraham P. Conan, and Lynn Davison. Philadelphia: Jewish Publication Society, 1969.

Campbell, Maria. *Halfbreed* (1973). Lincoln: University of Nebraska Press, 1982.

Carnegie, Andrew. *The Autobiography of Andrew Carnegie* (1920). Boston: Houghton Mifflin, 1920.

Casanova, Giovanni Giacomo. *Memoirs* (written 1789–1798; first complete publication, in the original French, 1826–1838). *History of my Life* (1966–1971). 12 vols. Trans. Willard R. Trask. New York: Harcourt, Brace, 1966–1971.

Cellini, Benvenuto. *The Autobiography* (written 1558–1566; first complete publication 1728). Trans. George Bull. New York: Penguin, 1956.

Chagall, Marc. *Ma vie* (1931). Trans. (from Russian) Bella Chagall. Paris: Stock, 1931.

Chaplin, Charlie. *My Autobiography* (1964). New York: Simon and Schuster, 1964.

Chessman, Caryl. *Cell 2455, Death Row* (1954). Englewood Cliffs, N.J.: Prentice-Hall, 1960.

Chona, Maria. *The Autobiography of a Papago Woman* (1936). With the collaboration of Ruth Underhill. New York: Holt, Rinehart and Winston, 1979.

Churchill, Winston. *My Early Life* (1930; Churchill was awarded the Nobel Prize in Literature in 1953). London: Cooper, 1989.

———. *Thoughts and Adventures* (1932). London: Macmillan, 1942.

Cleaver, Eldridge. *Soul on Ice* (1968). New York: Dell, 1968.

Clemens, Samuel. *The Autobiography of Mark Twain* (Clemens began to write autobiographical sketches in 1873, and he continued to experiment with the form until the end of his life in 1910; some of this material was first published in 1924). Ed. Charles Neider. New York: Harper, 1959.

Coleridge, Samuel Taylor. *Biographia Literaria* (1817). 2 vols. London: Oxford University Press, 1967.

Colette. *La maison de Claudine* (1922); *Sido* (1929); *Journal à rebours* (1941); *Paris de ma fênetre* (1944); *L'étoile vesper* (1946); *Le fanal bleu* (1949). These books have been published in English translation and are anthologized in *Earthly Paradise: An Autobiography*, ed. Robert Phelps, trans. Herma Briffault et al. New York: Farrar, Straus and Giroux, 1966.

Conroy, Frank. *Stop-Time* (1967). New York: Viking, 1967.

Cowley, Malcolm. *And I Worked at the Writer's Trade: Chapters of Literary History, 1918–1978* (1978; National Book Award). New York: Viking, 1978.

Croce, Benedetto. *An Autobiography* (1916). Trans. R. G. Collingwood. New York: Oxford University Press, 1926.

Dante. *La Vita Nuova* (ca. 1294). Trans. Barbara Reynolds. New York: Penguin, 1969.

Darrow, Clarence. *The Story of My Life* (1932). New York: Scribners, 1960.

Darwin, Charles. *Autobiography* (written 1876; additions made 1878 and 1881; published 1887). Ed. Gavin de Beer. New York: Oxford University Press, 1983.

Davis, Angela. *Angela Davis: An Autobiography* (1974). New York: Random, 1974.

de Beauvoir, Simone. *All Said and Done* (1972). Trans. Patrick O'Brian. New York: Putnam, 1974.

———. *The Coming of Age* (1970). Trans. Patrick O'Brian. New York: Putnam, 1972.

———. *Force of Circumstance* (1963). Trans. Richard Howard. New York: Putnam, 1965.

———. *Memoirs of a Dutiful Daughter* (1958). Trans. James Kirkup. New York: Harper and Row, 1974.

———. *The Prime of Life* (1960). Trans. Peter Green. New York: Penguin, 1962.

———. *A Very Easy Death* (1964). Trans. Patrick O'Brian. New York: Pantheon, 1965.

De Quincey, Thomas. *Confessions of an English Opium Eater* (1822). Oxford: Oxford University Press, 1985.

Descartes, René. *Discourse on Method* (1637). Trans. F. E. Sutcliffe. Baltimore, Md.: Penguin, 1968.

Didion, Joan. *The White Album* (1979). New York: Simon and Schuster, 1979.

Dillard, Annie. *An American Childhood* (1987). New York: Harper and Row, 1987.

———. *Pilgrim at Tinker Creek* (1974). New York: Harpers Press, 1974.

———. *Teaching a Stone to Talk: Expeditions and Encounters* (1982). New York: Harper and Row, 1982.

———. *The Writing Life* (1989). New York: Harper and Row, 1989.

Dinesen, Isak. *Out of Africa* (1937). New York: Modern Library, 1952.

Douglass, Frederick. *Life and Times of Frederick Douglass* (1881; revised edition 1892). New York: Collier, 1962.

———. *My Bondage and My Freedom* (1855). New York: Dover, 1969.

———. *Narrative of the Life of Frederick Douglass, an American Slave, Written by Himself* (1845). New York: Signet, 1968.

Duberman, Martin. *Cures: A Gay Man's Odyssey* (1991). New York: Dutton, 1991.

Du Bois, W. E. B. *The Autobiography of W. E. B. DuBois: A Soliloquy on Viewing My Life from the Last Decade of Its First Century* (1968). New York: International, 1968.

———. *Darkwater: Voices from within the Veil* (1921). New York: Harcourt Brace, 1921.

———. *Dusk of Dawn: An Essay toward an Autobiography of a Race Concept* (1940). New York: Harcourt Brace, 1940.

Duncan, Isadora. *My Life* (1927). New York: Liveright, 1955.

Dyson, Freeman. *Disturbing the Universe* (1979). New York: Harper and Row, 1979.

Eastman, Charles A. (Ohiyesa). *From the Deep Woods to Civilization: Chapters in the Autobiography of an Indian* (1916). Lincoln: University of Nebraska Press, 1977.

———. *Indian Boyhood* (1902). New York: Dover, 1971.

Edwards, Jonathan. *Personal Narrative* (written ca. 1740; published 1765). In *Basic Writings*, ed. Ola Elizabeth Winslow. New York: Signet, 1966.

Eisenstein, Sergei. *Immoral Memories* (written 1946–1948; published 1964). Trans. Herbert Marshall. Boston: Houghton Mifflin, 1983.

Feynman, Richard. *Surely You're Joking, Mr. Feynman!: Adventures of a Curious Character* (1985). New York: Norton, 1985.

Fitzgerald, F. Scott. *The Crack-Up* (1945). Compiled by Edmund Wilson. New York: New Directions, 1964.

Flanner, Janet. *Paris Journal: 1944–1965* (1965; National Book Award). New York: Atheneum, 1965.

———. *Paris Journal: 1965–1971* (1971). New York: Atheneum, 1971.

Frank, Anne. *The Diary of a Young Girl* (written 1942–1944; published 1947). New York: Pocket Books, 1953.

Frankl, Viktor E. *Man's Search for Meaning* (1946). Rev. ed. New York: Pocket Books, 1984.

Franklin, Benjamin. *Autobiography* (written 1771–1790; first complete publication 1868). Ed. J. A. Leo Lemay and P. M. Zall. New York: Norton, 1986.

Freud, Sigmund. *An Autobiographical Study* (1925). Trans. and ed. James Strachey. New York: Norton, 1989.

Fukuzawa, Yukichi. *Autobiography* (1899). Rev. trans. Eiichi Kiyooka. New York: Columbia University Press, 1966.

Gandhi, Mohandas. *An Autobiography: The Story of My Experiments with Truth* (1929). Trans. Mahadev Desai. Boston: Beacon, 1957.

Garland, Hamlin. *A Son of the Middle Border* (1917). New York: Macmillan, 1962.

Genet, Jean. *The Thief's Journal* (1949). Trans. Bernard Frechtman. New York: Grove, 1964.

Gibbon, Edward. *Memoirs of My Life* (1796). Ed. Betty Radice. New York: Penguin, 1984.

Gide, André. *If It Die* (private printing 1920; published 1924; Gide was awarded the Nobel Prize in Literature in 1947). Trans. Dorothy Bussy. New York: Random, 1935.

Giovanni, Nikki. *Gemini: An Extended Autobiographical Statement on My First Twenty-One Years of Being a Black Poet* (1971). Indianapolis, Ind.: Bobbs, Merrill, 1971.

Goethe, von, Johann Wolfgang. *Poetry and Truth* (1833). Trans. John Oxenford. New York: Horizon Press, 1969.

Goldman, Emma. *Living My Life* (1931). 2 vols. New York: Dover, 1970.

Gorky, Maxim. *My Childhood* (1914); *In the World* (1916); *My Universities* (1923). Collected in *The Autobiography of Maxim Gorky*. Trans. Isidor Schneider. Secaucus, N.J.: Citadel Press, 1949.

Gosse, Edmund. *Father and Son: A Study of Two Temperaments* (published anonymously in 1907). New York: Norton, 1963.

Grant, Ulysses S. *Personal Memoirs of Ulysses S. Grant* (1886). New York: Library of America, 1990.

Grass, Günter, *Show Your Tongue* (1988). Trans. John E. Woods. New York: Harcourt Brace, 1989.

Guthrie, Woody. *Bound for Glory* (1943). New York: Signet, 1970.

Hayslip, Le Ly. *When Heaven and Earth Changed Places: A Vietnamese Woman's Journey from War to Peace* (1989). New York: Plume, 1990.

Haywood, William. *Bill Haywood's Book: The Autobiography of William D. Haywood* (1929). New York: International, 1929.

Hecht, Ben. *A Child of the Century* (1954). New York: Simon and Schuster, 1954.

Hellman, Lillian. *Pentimento* (1973). Boston: Little, Brown, 1973.

———. *Scoundrel Time* (1976). New York: Bantam, 1977.

———. *An Unfinished Woman: A Memoir* (1969; National Book Award). Boston: Little, Brown, 1969.

Herr, Michael. *Dispatches* (1977). New York: Avon, 1978.

Hoffman, Abbie. *Soon to Be a Major Motion Picture* (1980). New York: Putnam, 1980.

Hopkins, Sarah Winnemucca. *Life among the Piutes: Their Wrongs and Claims* (1883). Bishop, Calif.: Sierra Media, 1969.

Howells, William Dean. *A Boy's Town* (1890). Included in Howells, *Selected Writings*, ed. Henry Steele Commager. New York: Random, 1950.

———. *Years of My Youth* (1916). Bloomington: Indiana University Press, 1975.

Hugo, Victor. *Contemplations* (1856). Ed. Léon Cellier. Paris: Garnier, 1969.

Hurston, Zora Neale. *Dust Tracks on a Road: An Autobiography* (1942). Urbana: University of Illinois Press, 1984.

Huston, John. *An Open Book* (1980). New York: Knopf, 1980.

Iacocca, Lee, with William Novak. *Iacocca: An Autobiography* (1984). New York: Bantam, 1984.

Ignatius of Loyola, Saint. *The Autobiography of St. Ignatius Loyola* (1555). Trans. Joseph F. O'Callaghan. New York: Harper and Row, 1974.

Jacobs, Harriet. *Incidents in the Life of a Slave Girl* (1861). Detroit, Mich.: Negro History Press, 1969.

James, Henry. *A Small Boy and Others* (1913); *Notes of a Son and Brother* (1914); *The Middle Years* (1917). Collected in *Autobiography* (1956). Ed. Frederick W. Dupee. London: Allen, 1956.

Jefferson, Thomas. *The Autobiography* (written 1821; published 1829). In Jefferson, *Writings*. New York: Library of America, 1984.

Jung, Carl. *Memories, Dreams, Reflections* (1961). Ed. Aniela Jaffé. Trans. Richard and Clara Winston. New York: Vintage, 1963.

Kang, Younghill. *East Goes West* (1937). New York: Scribners, 1937.

Kazin, Alfred. *A Walker in the City* (1951). New York: Harcourt Brace, 1951.

Keller, Helen. *The Story of My Life* (1905). Garden City, N.Y.: Doubleday, 1954.

Kempe, Margery. *The Book of Margery Kempe* (transcribed between 1432 and 1436). Trans. Barry Windeatt. New York: Penguin, 1985.

Kennan, George F. *Memoirs: 1925–1950* (1967; National Book Award and Pulitzer Prize). Boston: Little, Brown, 1967.

———. *Memoirs: 1950–1963* (1972). Boston: Little, Brown, 1972.

Kingston, Maxine Hong. *China Men* (1980; National Book Award). New York: Knopf, 1980.

———. *The Woman Warrior: Memoirs of a Girlhood among Ghosts* (1976). New York: Vintage, 1989.

Kissinger, Henry. *White House Years*. (1979; National Book Award). Boston: Little, Brown, 1979.

Kittredge, William. *Hole in the Sky* (1992). New York: Knopf, 1992.

Kogawa, Joy. *Obasan* (1981). Boston: Godine, 1982.

Kovic, Ron. *Born on the Fourth of July* (1976). New York: Pocket Books, 1977.

Kurosawa, Akira. *Something Like an Autobiography* (1982). Trans. Audie E. Bock. New York: Vintage, 1983.

Lame Deer, John. *Lame Deer: Seeker of Visions* (1972). With the collaboration of Richard Erdoes. New York: Simon and Schuster, 1972.

Lawrence, T. E. *Seven Pillars of Wisdom* (1935). London: Cape, 1973.

Leduc, Violette. *La Bâtarde* (1964). Trans. Derek Coltman. New York: Farrar, Straus and Giroux, 1965.

————. *La Chasse à l'Amour* (1973). Paris: Gallimard, 1973.

————. *Mad in Pursuit* (1970). Trans. Derek Coltman. New York: Farrar, Straus and Giroux, 1971.

Leiris, Michel. *Manhood: A Journey from Childhood into the Fierce Order of Virility* (1946). Trans. Richard Howard. New York: Grossman, 1963.

Levi, Carlo. *Christ Stopped at Eboli: The Story of a Year* (1947). Trans. Frances Frenaye. New York: Farrar, Straus and Giroux, 1963.

Lévi-Strauss, Claude. *Tristes Tropiques* (1955). Trans. John and Doreen Weightman. New York: Atheneum, 1974.

Lewis, Oscar. *The Children of Sanchez: Autobiography of a Mexican Family* (1961). New York: Random, 1961.

Lifton, Betty Jean. *Twice Born: Memoirs of an Adopted Daughter* (1975). New York: Penguin, 1977.

Lowe, Pardee. *Father and Glorious Descendant* (1943). Boston: Little, Brown, 1943.

McCarthy, Mary. *Memories of a Catholic Girlhood* (1957). New York: Harcourt Brace, 1957.

Mailer, Norman. *The Armies of the Night* (1968; National Book Award). New York: Signet, 1968.

Malcolm X. *The Autobiography of Malcolm X* (1965). Reported by Alex Haley. New York: Grove, 1966.

Malraux, André. *Anti-Memoirs* (1967). Trans. Terence Kilmartin. New York: Holt, Rinehart and Winston, 1968.

Marcus Aurelius. *Meditations* [*To Myself*] (written 171–180). Trans. Maxwell Staniforth. New York: Penguin, 1964.

Mead, Margaret. *Blackberry Winter: My Earlier Years* (1972). New York: Morrow, 1972.

Merton, Thomas. *The Seven Storey Mountain* (1948). New York: Harcourt Brace, 1948.

Mezzrow, Milton. *Really the Blues* (1946). New York: Random, 1946.

Mill, John Stuart. *Autobiography* (1873). New York: Signet, 1964.

Miller, Henry. *Tropic of Cancer* (1934). New York: Grove, 1961.

Momaday, N. Scott. *The Names: A Memoir* (1976). Tucson: University of Arizona Press, 1976.

————. *The Way to Rainy Mountain* (1969). New York: Ballantine, 1973.

Monette, Paul. *Becoming a Man: Half a Life Story* (1992; National Book Award). New York: Harcourt Brace, 1992.

————. *Borrowed Time: An AIDS Memoir* (1988). New York: Harcourt Brace, 1988.

Montaigne, Michel de. *Essays* (written 1572–1588; published in five editions before his death in 1592). Trans. Donald M. Frame. Stanford, Calif.: Stanford University Press, 1958.

Moody, Anne. *Coming of Age in Mississippi* (1968). New York: Dell, 1968.

Moraga, Cherríe. *Loving in the War Years* (1983). Boston: South End Press, 1983.

Mountain Wolf Woman. *Mountain Wolf Woman, Sister of Crashing Thunder* (1961). Ed. Nancy Oestreich Lurie. Ann Arbor: University of Michigan Press, 1961.

Muir, John. *The Story of My Boyhood and Youth* (1913). New York: Houghton Mifflin, 1913.

Mura, David. *Turning Japanese: Memoirs of a Sansei* (1991). New York: Anchor, 1992.

Nabokov, Vladimir. *Speak, Memory: An Autobiography Revisited* (1967). New York: Pyramid Books, 1968.

Newman, John Henry, Cardinal. *Apologia Pro Vita Sua* (1864). Ed. David J. DeLaura. New York: Norton, 1968.

Nietzsche, Friedrich. *Ecce Homo: How One Becomes What One Is* (written 1888; published 1908). Trans. Walter Kaufmann. New York: Vintage, 1967.

O'Casey, Sean. *I Knock at the Door* (1939); *Pictures in the Hallway* (1942); *Drums under the Windows* (1945); *Inishfallen, Fare Thee Well* (1949); *Rose and Crown* (1952); *Sunset and Evening Star* (1954). Collected in *Autobiographies* (1963). 2 vols. New York: Carroll and Graf, 1984.

Orozco, José Clemente. *Autobiografía* (1945). Mexico: Edicions Era, 1970.

Pasternak, Boris. *I Remember: Sketch for an Autobiography* (1959; Pasternak was awarded the Nobel Prize in Literature in 1958). Trans. David Magarshack. New York: Meridian, 1960.

——. *Safe Conduct* (1931). Trans. Beatrice Scott. In *Selected Writings*. New York: New Directions, 1949.

Pirsig, Robert M. *Lila: An Inquiry into Morals* (1991). New York: Bantam, 1991.

——. *Zen and the Art of Motorcycle Maintenance: An Inquiry into Values* (1974). New York: Bantam, 1984.

Pretty-Shield. *Pretty-Shield: Medicine Woman of the Crows* (1932). With the collaboration of Frank B. Linderman. Lincoln: University of Nebraska Press, 1974.

Ray, Man. *Self-Portrait* (1963). Boston: Little, Brown, 1963.

Reik, Theodor. *Listening with the Third Ear: The Inner Experience of a Psychoanalyst* (1948). New York: Arena, 1972.

Renoir, Jean. *My Life and My Films* (1974). Trans. Norman Denny. New York: Atheneum, 1974.

Riis, Jacob. *The Making of an American* (1903). New York: Macmillan, 1970.

Robeson, Paul. *Here I Stand* (1958). Boston: Beacon, 1971.

Rodriguez, Richard. *Days of Obligation: An Argument with My Mexican Father* (1992). New York: Viking, 1992.

————. *Hunger of Memory: The Education of Richard Rodriguez* (1982). New York: Bantam, 1983.

Rousseau, Jean-Jacques. *The Confessions* (written 1766–1770; first complete publication 1788). Trans. J. M. Cohen. New York: Penguin, 1954.

Ruskin, John. *Praeterita* (written and published 1885–1889; left unfinished). New York: Oxford University Press, 1978.

Russell, Bertrand. *The Autobiography of Bertrand Russell* (1967–1969; Russell was awarded the Nobel Prize in Literature in 1950). 3 vols. London: Allen and Unwin, 1967–1969.

Sachs, Maurice. *Witches' Sabbath* (written in the 1940s; published 1960). Trans. Richard Howard. New York: Stein and Day, 1964.

Sand, George. *My Life* (1854–1855). Abridged and trans. Dan Hofstadter. New York: Harper and Row, 1979.

Sanger, Margaret. *An Autobiography* (1938). New York: Dover, 1971.

Sartre, John-Paul. *The Words* (1964; awarded the Nobel Prize in Literature in 1964, Sartre declined to accept it). Trans. Bernard Frechtman. New York: Fawcett, 1964.

Seneca. *Letters from a Stoic* (ca. 63–65). Trans. Robin Campbell. New York: Penguin, 1969.

Shaw, Nate. *All God's Dangers: The Life of Nate Shaw* (1974; National Book Award). Reported by Theodore Rosengarten. New York: Knopf, 1974.

Silko, Leslie. *Storyteller* (1981). New York: Seaver, 1981.

Smedley, Agnes. *Daughter of Earth* (1929). Old Westbury, N.Y.: Feminist Press, 1973.

Socrates. *Apology* (399 B.C.). In Plato, *The Last Days of Socrates*. Trans. Hugh Tredennick. New York: Penguin, 1969.

Soyinka, Wole. *Aké: The Years of Childhood* (1981; Soyinka was awarded the Nobel Prize in Literature in 1986). New York: Random, 1981.

————. *The Man Died: Prison Notes* (1972). London: Rex Collings, 1972.

Spender, Stephen. *World within World* (1951). New York: Harcourt Brace, 1951.

Standing Bear, Luther. *My Indian Boyhood* (1931). New York: Houghton Mifflin, 1931.

————. *My People the Sioux* (1928). Lincoln: University of Nebraska Press, 1975.

Stanton, Elizabeth Cady. *Eighty Years and More: Reminiscences, 1815–1897* (1898). New York: Schocken, 1971.

Steffens, Lincoln. *The Autobiography* (1931). 2 vols. New York: Harcourt Brace, 1958.

Stein, Gertrude. *The Autobiography of Alice B. Toklas* (1933). In *The Selected Writings of Gertrude Stein*, ed. Carl Van Vechten. New York: Vintage, 1962.

————. *Everybody's Autobiography* (1937). New York: Vintage, 1973.

Stendhal. *The Life of Henry Brulard* (1890; published posthumously). Trans. Jean Stewart and B. C. J. G. Knight. New York: Noonday, 1958.

————. *Memoirs of an Egotist* (1892; published posthumously). Trans. David Ellis. New York: Horizon Press, 1975.

Stravinsky, Igor. *Chroniques de ma vie* (1935). Paris: Denoeel/Gonthier, 1962.

Sullivan, Louis. *The Autobiography of an Idea* (1924). New York: Dover, 1957.

Sun, Yat-sen. *Memoirs of a Chinese Revolutionary: A Programme of National Reconstruction for China* (1918). Taipei: China Cultural Service, 1953.

Talayesva, Don C. *Sun Chief: The Autobiography of a Hopi Indian* (1942). With the collaboration of Leo W. Simmons. New Haven: Yale University Press, 1974.

Teresa of Ávila, Saint. *The Life of Teresa of Jesus* (1565). Trans. and ed. E. Allison Peers. Garden City, N.Y.: Image Books, 1960.

Thomas, Piri. *Down These Mean Streets* (1967). New York: Knopf, 1967.

Thoreau, Henry David. *Walden* (1854). Ed. Owen Thomas. New York: Norton, 1966.

Toklas, Alice B. *What Is Remembered* (1963). New York: Holt, Rinehart and Winston, 1963.

Toyoda, Eiji. *Toyota: Fifty Years in Motion, An Autobiography by the Chairman* (1985). New York: Kodansha International, 1987.

Trotsky, Leon. *My Life: An Attempt at an Autobiography* (1930). New York: Scribners, 1930.

Two Leggings. *Two Leggings: The Making of a Crow Warrior* (interviews conducted by William Wildschut 1919–1923). With the collaboration of Peter Nabokov. New York: Crowell, 1967.

Valéry, Paul. *Moi* (a selection of autobiographical pieces written between 1890 and 1944, a year before his death). Trans. Marthiel and Jackson Mathews. Princeton, N.J.: Princeton University Press, 1975.

Vico, Giambattista. *Autobiography* (written 1725–1731; published in 1728 and 1731). Trans. T. G. Bergin and M. H. Fisch. Ithaca, N.Y.: Cornell University Press, 1983.

Washington, Booker T. *Up from Slavery: An Autobiography* (1901). New York: Dodd, Mead, 1965.

Watts, Alan. *In My Own Way: An Autobiography, 1915–1965* (1972). New York: Pantheon, 1972.

Weil, Simone. *Waiting for God* (1950). Trans. Emma Craufurd. New York: Harper and Row, 1951.

Wells, H. G. *Experiment in Autobiography* (1934). New York: Macmillan, 1934.

Welty, Eudora. *One Writer's Beginnings* (1984). Cambridge: Harvard University Press, 1985.

West, Mae. *Goodness Had Nothing to Do with It: Autobiography* (1959). Englewood Cliffs, N.J.: Prentice-Hall, 1959.

Whitman, Walt. *Leaves of Grass* (published first in 1855, this book of poems was enlarged during 10 editions over Whitman's lifetime). In *Complete Poetry and Selected Prose,* ed. James E. Miller, Jr. Boston: Houghton, Mifflin, 1959.

Wilde, Oscar. *De Profundis* (written 1895–1897; published 1905). New York: Vintage Books, 1964.

Williams, William Carlos. *The Autobiography* (1951). New York: New Directions, 1967.

Wilson, Edmund. *Upstate: Records and Recollections of Northern New York* (1971). New York: Farrar, Straus and Giroux, 1971.

Wong, Jade Snow. *Fifth Chinese Daughter* (1945). New York: Harper, 1950.

Wordsworth, William. *The Prelude, or Growth of a Poet's Mind* (1805). Ed. Ernest de Selincourt and Stephen Gill. New York: Oxford University Press, 1970.

———. *The Prelude, or Growth of a Poet's Mind* (1850). New York: Oxford University Press, 1970.

Wright, Frank Lloyd. *An Autobiography* (1943). New York: Horizon Press, 1977.

Wright, Richard. *American Hunger* (1945). New York: Harper and Row, 1977.

———. *Black Boy: A Record of Childhood and Youth* (1945). New York: Harper and Row, 1966.

Yeats, William Butler. *Reveries over Childhood and Youth* (1916); *The Trembling of the Veil* (1922; Yeats was awarded the Nobel Prize in Literature in 1923); *Dramatis Personae* (1935). Collected in *Autobiography* (1944). New York: Collier, 1965.

Yogananda, Paramahansa. *Autobiography of a Yogi* (1946). Los Angeles, Calif.: Self-Realization Fellowship, 1972.

Zweig, Stefan. *The World of Yesterday* (1943). Lincoln: University of Nebraska Press, 1964.

INDEX

Material in the Bibliographic Essay is not listed here.

About the Author

James Goodwin teaches in the Department of English at the University of California, Los Angeles. His articles on autobiography have appeared in the volume *Critical Essays on Henry Miller* and in the journals *Genre, ESQ: A Journal of the American Renaissance, Denver Quarterly,* and *Biography.* In film studies, his other primary area of research, Professor Goodwin has published *Eisenstein, Cinema, and History* (1993) and *Akira Kurosawa and Intertextual Cinema* (1993).